The Open Door

Miriam Blackwell's account of
The Salvation Army's
second entry into
Russia and
The Commonwealth of Independent States

United Kingdom Territory of The Salvation Army
101 Newington Causeway, London SE1 6BN

© The General of The Salvation Army 2001
First published in the United Kingdom in 2001
ISBN 0 85412 690 2

Miriam Blackwell served in Russia/Commonwealth of Independent States from 1993 to 1996. During that time she was responsible for setting up and heading the command's Resource Centre in Moscow.

Previous to this, for many years, she was a teacher in primary schools until she became head of the Schools Information Service at IHQ. Work in the Editorial Department followed, during which Miriam was an editorial assistant on *The War Cry* and the then *YS* (*The Young Soldier*). In retirement, Miriam worked at the International Heritage Centre.

At her home corps, Catford in South London, she had served as young people's sergeant-major, and also worked with guides and brownies. Miriam was promoted to Glory in 1999, quite soon after her retirement.

Cover artwork by Misha Gavrilov
Cover design by Major Bruce Tulloch
Typeset by THQ Print and Design Unit
Produced by THQ Literary Unit
Printed by Page Bros (Norwich) Ltd

CONTENTS

INTRODUCTION

THIS account springs from the experience of the author and the testimony of Salvationist colleagues who witnessed these events. It has been gleaned from both the written and spoken word during the time of uneasy change with which the 20th century drew to a close.

It is a story of vision and determination, prayer and courage, hope and despair. In this story, those who are not named are as important as those who played a more prominent role. Events not recorded here are also vital parts of The Salvation Army's ministry, waiting to be told as an inspiration for God's people. It is a continuing story, for until the end of time Jesus, who said 'I am the door', will be offering boundless salvation to all who come to him.

Our prayer is that the fine Salvationists of Russia and the Commonwealth of Independent States may continue to find mercy, grace and peace in Jesus Christ and serve him faithfully to the end.

PROLOGUE

THE Moscow metro train drew into the station in the Presnya district. Before the doors were fully open passengers stumbled out, pushing through the alleyway of waiting travellers. No sooner had a space in the compartment been vacated than another person squeezed into it, such was the crush. It was all very normal.

But the passengers who squeezed into one compartment were not normal. For one thing they were smiling and talking, breaking the standard sombre silence of the underground. Young and old, men and women, they seemed to have something warm about them which began to thaw the surrounding atmosphere. People glanced up curiously. Some of the newcomers were wearing uniform – not unusual in Russia where thousands of men were in military and police forces. A second glance showed that on this uniform a complex cap badge displaced the usual red star, and the words on the red band proclaimed *Armiya Spasseniya* – The Salvation Army. Here was yet another new thing among the many confusions which perestroika had brought.

'What is The Salvation Army?' One man voiced the question everyone was asking with their eyes. The uniformed man strap-hanging close by was quick to answer. Each day he travelled to work in uniform, ready to take every opportunity to increase awareness of the organisation which had come to mean so much to him and his friends. Quickly, sincerely, he explained that he belonged to an international Christian Protestant Church. Members of the Movement had come from Norway in 1990 as soon as new legislation allowed them to enter Russia. Now, three years later, there were Russian pastors teaching the gospel of Jesus Christ and showing their faith by active social concern in the community.

'Russian leaders in a new Protestant church?' queried the man, who was aware of many Western Christian missions having hit major cities in brief, highly-publicised events. He hadn't realised that some of the seed planted then was already firmly rooted in Russian soil. 'Yes!' replied the Salvationist. 'And this isn't the first time The Salvation Army has been in Russia, either!'

With that tantalising remark the conversation had to close. The train halted, the doors opened, and the tide of pushing people ebbed and flowed urgently so that Moscow could continue moving with no delay. Contact with the group of Salvationists, brief as it may have been, had set a number of people thinking. Some remembered seeing the homeless queuing at a station for soup served by members of this Army. Others had caught glimpses of its humanitarian work on TV programmes. Most of the impressions were good, kind, encouraging – just the sort of feelings created by the cheerful people who had left the compartment. Over all else was a feeling of hope.

The Salvationists were especially buoyed up with hope by the meeting they had just attended. In the Presnya Culture Palace, not far from the White House, Russia's parliament headquarters, a new group of young men and women had been welcomed to begin training for leadership in The Salvation Army. Russian? Yes – and Ukrainian, Moldovan, and Georgian. God's Holy Spirit was working in many parts of the Commonwealth of Independent States, building up The Salvation Army. Countless people longed for their country to experience the invigorating wind of God blowing through newly-opening doors. They saw in The Salvation Army a special style of Christian ministry which would work.

Make no mistake, God had been at work inside the huge Soviet State throughout the time it was locked away from the rest of the world. The Orthodox Church, persecuted, split, used and recognised in turn by Communist authorities, had been shaken to its ancient foundations but still stood. Baptists met in secret and endured great discrimination and suffering. Other denominations, like The Salvation Army, were pushed out. Faithful members were exiled or isolated.

The silent faith of generations of babushkas – old grandmothers – had kept alight a tiny flame in many families. Bible truths committed to memory survived when the printed word was confiscated and burned. A thousand years of Christian influence had rooted deeply. For 70 years it had been buried in darkness. Now it was as if the Saviour of the world, crucified and buried outside the city gates, had once again risen to life.

This story tells how Russian, Ukrainian, Moldovan and Georgian people have discovered William Booth's Army, and are faithfully doing their part to win the world for Jesus. In print, the story will never be complete. For every piece of evidence of the Holy Spirit's work recounted in these pages there are many more to which others could testify. For every person named, there are hundreds who also deserve a mention. We may not know their names, but they are recognised by the Good Shepherd as he leads them through the door into the safety of his fold.

Chapter 1

A FOOT IN THE DOOR

The Salvation Army's Russian overture

EUROPEAN nations have had close family ties for hundreds of years. Ever since men ventured out of their safe tribal areas to seek their fortunes, ideas, inventions, commodities and fashions have forged links to bring them together. At times these were like iron, binding groups forcefully as a result of a strong man's greedy ambition. At other times the links created bonds of friendship and respect.

The great Russian nation, straddling Europe and Asia, was part of this process. Because of its vast size and tough terrain, Western culture had taken root only in the cities. In the 1860s, when William Booth found his destiny among London's impoverished East Enders, Russian peasants were struggling to gain rights legally granted in 1861, freeing them from feudal serfdom. Cultural links were important to the poor of neither Britain nor Russia. Hunger and homelessness were their common bond – unlikely as they were to have been aware of counterparts half a world away, cut off by confining circumstances.

As The Salvation Army's work began to impact the human melting pot of East London, another ingredient was added. Driven by persecution, thousands of Russian Jews sought refuge in that city. By the end of the century more than 80,000 Russians and

Russian Poles were living in England in small communities. Many of these were crowded into the East End, scratching a living by such enterprises as trading old clothes. Perhaps this was why William Booth added Russia to the list of countries to be stormed by his 'Army without guns'. For the moment though, there was no friendly opening for even a peaceful army. Protestant churches, indigenous ones included, were not welcomed by the hierarchy of the Orthodox Church naturally clinging to a power-base established through nearly a thousand years.

However, the printed word often penetrates and influences where human contact is prevented. Years before The Salvation Army was active in Russia, the Russian censor approved Salvation Army publications. A three-line report in the British *War Cry* dated 25 February 1888 concludes, 'Russia is, therefore, now open for our literature.' Army writers had the opportunity to disseminate the gospel, fashioning a key with which to unlock the door.

The ideas of General Booth were soon sown in the Russian Empire. Three years later *The Glasgow Herald* reported that these ideas had taken deep root in St Petersburg (in 1914 to be renamed Petrograd, then in 1924, Leningrad, reverting to St Petersburg in 1991). But at the beginning of 1891 the Orthodox Church was alerted to this intrusion, seeing it as a threat.

Commissioner George Scott Railton, described by William Booth's son, Bramwell, as having a restless, fearless spirit, was later to knock at the forbidding door. During a six-month tour of Europe in 1904 he visited St Petersburg, then the Russian capital, and had a vision of Salvation Army troops marching along Nevsky Prospekt on a God-given mission of love to this struggling nation.

Five years later *The War Cry* of 9 January 1909 carried a short but significant report: Commissioner Railton had again spent several weeks in Russia. During that visit he led crowded meetings in St Petersburg and made contact with many people of the ruling class. Tsar Nicholas himself, however, politely but firmly declined Railton's requests for an audience.

As Railton recounted his experiences to William Booth the conviction that the Army's entry to Russia should be a priority in his plans was confirmed. The Founder was recovering from eye surgery. At the age of 80 this was a risky procedure but he was already rapidly regaining strength when a *War Cry* representative interviewed him about his plans for 1909.

'Russia at the present moment is certainly to the front, and must be entered at the earliest moment at which plans can be made,' said Booth. 'Our delay can only be excused because of the gigantic difficulties which have barred the way. But, in the most remarkable manner, the door seems to be opening, slowly, it may be, but, I still think surely.'

In March, keen to assess the situation for himself, the elderly William Booth made the tiring journey to Russia. Scarcely had he stepped out of the train than he was met by a colonel of the Russian Army. This official had come not to deter, but to encourage the Salvationists. He expressed appreciation of the Army's work and wished them success in Russia.

A detailed report of the visit was filed in *The War Cry* of 10 April 1909 in which this positive attitude was found time and time again. A countess sent a motor car to take the General to his hotel. A philanthropist, Miss Von Weissberg, urged him to commence work, offering her support. Count Pahlin and Baron Nikolai, also known for their active concern, spoke about the conditions of the poor, confirming that the opportunity was ripe for the Army to commence operations. The British Ambassador received the General and expressed sympathetic interest. Senator Messeyedov spoke of his daughter who was serving as a Salvation Army officer in Paris. These people and others echoed the Macedonian call, 'Come over and help us!'

In spite of widespread accusations that the Russian nobility was unconcerned about the plight of the poor, only recently released from serfdom, *The War Cry* reported evidence of many who were involved in charitable societies and social institutions. What was lacking was the skill which came from experience. Russians who had travelled abroad recognised that William Booth's Army could offer this skill in the light of 40 years of Christian social service in different parts of the world.

Like Railton, Booth failed to gain entry to the palace, although he was allowed to attend a session of the Duma, being seated in the Diplomatic Circle. This parliament was only the third elected governing body the country had known – a vulnerable infant in democratic terms.

Perhaps as Booth listened to the speech delivered by the Minister of Commerce he recalled his youthful involvement with the Chartist movement in Britain. Here in Russia were similar struggles as the repressed peasant class fought for rights against the despotic Tsar and his autocratic advisers. Clearly there was a need for the social gospel the Army could bring. Colonel and Mrs Jens Povlsen, fine Danish officers, moved into St Petersburg, ready for action. They applied for registration straight away.

In the city were wealthy Christians who saw a way forward. The Salvation Army had improved living conditions through Christian action in many other countries. Colonel and Mrs Povlsen should have every encouragement to do the same in Russia. Supporters gave money and even allowed them the use of a hall. People crowded into the meetings week by week. Their spiritual hunger was as acute as their physical need and many found sustenance in the gospel message.

Determined as they were to obey God's commission, the Povlsens knew they were courting danger. Such public work would not go unnoticed by those who were ordered to root out illegal activity.

As often happens, bureaucrats were not keen to facilitate the acceptance of new ideas with foreign connections. Time passed. In 1912, the Povlsens received a reply to their application to commence the Army's work. It was negative. William Booth died that year knowing that the door of Russia was for the moment firmly closed, if not locked fast, against him and his Army. Yet the fact that the last change of leadership made by Booth before his death was the transfer of Colonel Karl Larsson from Sweden to Finland was to sound a significant rap on that firmly closed door.

Finland, where The Salvation Army had been active since 1889, was at this time dominated by her powerful neighbour, with a Russian governor-general in control of the small country.

Sharing the Founder's vision for Russia, Colonel Larsson began to search for a chink in the closed door as soon as he took up his new appointment.

When, in the spring of 1913, it was suggested by a State official that the Army should be represented at an international 'hygienic' exhibition in St Petersburg, Larsson saw the opening he was waiting for. Cleanliness being next to godliness, this virtue was always given its place in the Army's social services, which could now be portrayed in a display, giving Russian citizens some idea of the Army's role in the community. Its Christian motivation could be made clear by Salvationist stewards. Given the opportunity to answer questions from interested visitors, there were great possibilities.

Official permission for such an exhibit being received, at once work went ahead to prepare a presentation worthy of the occasion. The aim was to show how the Army in Finland was promoting national health, physically and morally. There was no shortage of evidence. The effective social work in Finland told its own story. A life-size model of a 'slum' officer, in starched white apron and broad-brimmed hat, stood guard over a typical hostel bed on which were displayed samples of needlework produced by women who had found safety and security in Army shelters. Photographs of various centres in Finland framed the scene.

An illustrated pamphlet was prepared in the Russian language. In addition to facts and figures, it contained a clear explanation of the religious foundations of the work on view. The exhibition certainly made an impact. Crowds of visitors went away with a clearer understanding of the Army's work and motivation. The organisers too were impressed – they awarded the exhibit first place in its section! The main entrance to the country was closed still, but a side door had opened a little and the Army had slipped inside.

Colonel Larsson observed and prayed, hoping the Army would be able to make the most of the tide of goodwill resulting from the success of the exhibition. Many wanted the Salvationists to stay, in spite of a Russian journalist expressing the hope that The Salvation Army would not send 'foreign agents' to the renamed Petrograd.

The Army's work took root and flourished in Russia, sometimes against impossible odds, for the next 10 years. The story of those years, of how *Vestnik Spasseniya – The War Cry –* was distributed by Finnish heralds, and the remarkable part played by a Russian Jew cannot be told here.

Suffice it to record here that *The Salvation Army Year Book* for 1924 does not list Russia as one of the 79 countries in which the Army was operating. The doors of that great country had swung firmly shut behind the few departing overseas officers. No longer could the uniform be seen in the mean back streets of Petrograd nor was *Vestnik Spasseniya* to be found in the hands of Moscovites. Refugee children in Vologda and Orel heard no more stories of Jesus, nor felt the warmth of his love in those who cared for them. This small Christian group, life to many and anathema to others, was no longer visible.

This did not mean, however, that it ceased to exist. Hidden in the hearts of countless people whose lives had been touched by the ministry of Salvationists, seeds of God's love had begun to germinate. Some shrivelled from dryness of spirit. Others were choked by thorns of evil. But, in spite of hostile conditions all around, there was fertile soil and here the fruits of love, joy, peace, patience and longsuffering were tasted.

Christians in Soviet Russia endured every degree of suffering. For some, it was suffering to be deprived of opportunities to worship and study God's word in their chosen way. For others, it meant betrayal, imprisonment, mental and physical torture, exile, deprivation and death.

After Lenin's death in 1924 the whole nation suffered as powerful men with opposing ideas and ideals struggled for supremacy. Determined to build the ideal State without outside help – and without God – Bolsheviks steamrollered over the very citizens they claimed would benefit.

As the Communist system took hold in Russia and its satellites, Stalin looked beyond Russia's borders to the rest of the world. So began a time when the fear and suspicion, which had become so much part of the process internally, grew to international proportions. Now all that Salvationists could do for Russia was to pray.

Chapter 2

TRACING A THREAD

The Army spirit survives final closure

WE shall never fully know the influence The Salvation Army had in the lives of men and women and boys and girls during the few short years the door was open into Russia but the Army press contains fascinating glimpses here and there.

A 1936 *All the World* article tells of 24-year-old Rachel Anishka, describing her enrolment as a Salvation Army soldier in Port Said. Her father, a new Christian, had attended Army meetings in Russia. He suffered imprisonment for his faith more than once. Finally he fled to Palestine, settling in Jerusalem with his family.

They attended a Christian mission and there Rachel committed her life to Christ. So great was her enthusiasm that her father was reminded of the Salvationists he had met long ago. This would be just the place for his daughter. He set about trying to contact the Army and at last a reply to his letter came from Germany, enclosed with a bundle of copies of *The War Cry*.

Her father was right. Rachel decided that this was her style as soon as she had absorbed the contents. Taking the papers she went to the cafes and markets of Jerusalem offering the good news to those who would listen and read.

Undaunted by indifference, even scorn, Rachel purchased papers, Army records and a red jersey with a yellow crest by post from England and continued her 'one woman Army' ministry for a number of years. How she longed to meet other Salvationists!

The first she ever met was Major Stannard, chaplain to British troops in Palestine. To her delight, friends arranged for him to visit her at the hospital where she was recovering from illness.

When General Evangeline Booth announced in *The War Cry* that pioneer officers, Adjutant and Mrs Underhill, were due to arrive in Port Said, Rachel wrote to them straight away. Eventually she met them when they came to Palestine for a short break. Arrangements were made for her to travel to Egypt and there, at a meeting of the new Port Said Corps, she was officially accepted as a Salvation Army soldier and charged to continue her witness at the geographical heart of Christianity.

A brief paragraph in a 1938 copy of *All the World* is a clue to Russian ministry in another distant corner – Shanghai. The book *Helps to Holiness* by Samuel Logan Brengle, which has taught so many about spiritual maturity, had been translated into Russian for the nurture of Russian Christians who had fled to that great Chinese port. (It was later reprinted in the 1990s and added to the resources available in Russia.)

A cadet in the 1946 session for officer-training in France was a Russian Jewess whose family had escaped there from persecution. A tantalisingly short report tells us that she had been rejected by her family on becoming a Christian. She found residential work nursing in an Army home in France and consequently became a Salvationist.

There are mentions of a Russian cadet entering the Army's London Training College from Paris long before that. Cadet Rogoff was commissioned as an officer in 1922, taking up an appointment in Portsmouth assisting Ensign and Mrs Robert Hoggard. After this, the trail goes cold. What happened to Captain Rogoff?

Many Salvation Army soldiers and a few officers remained behind the locked door, working out their faith whatever way that they could. They experienced great changes in town and country as the nation was moulded into the shape envisioned by its leaders.

Horrors of war came again, bringing unbelievable suffering in the cities of Moscow, Smolensk, Kiev and the now-named Leningrad (Petrograd) and Stalingrad (Volgograd), and devastation in rural areas where tanks rumbled in retribution.

Suspicion and fear marked post-Second-World-War days. Each great power jealously guarded its dreadful secrets. Travel abroad was out of the question for the average Russian citizen. After all, everything they needed – industry, the arts, holiday resorts, sport, even religion in its approved form – was available within the borders of the USSR. International organisations like The Salvation Army became just a faint memory kept alive in the minds of babushkas.

But for some elderly folk the Army meant more than a faint memory. It had been their life, and remained in them as an ache of bereavement. A Swedish visitor to Moscow was privileged to share this yearning one day in the 1950s. While resting on a park bench she was approached by a woman who had recognised her Christian lapel badge. No one else was near. It was safe to talk of these things. She introduced herself as Vera, carefully avoiding mention of her other name.

For two hours they conversed in basic Russian which the Swede could understand. The visitor heard how Vera's father, and then she herself, had been converted at The Salvation Army in Petrograd. She had worked with Salvation Army officers Karl Larsson, Arvid Zander and Helmy Boije and obviously remembered them well. Could this have been Vera Goronovitch, the first Russian to become an officer?

She told how when famine was severe in Petrograd in 1920 she went to relatives in the country, far away from any contact with the city, not returning until 1931 when the famine was not so severe but there was fear of a different kind in the city. It was unwise to make any enquiries about people who had disappeared.

Vera found a spiritual home in the Baptist Church until key members went missing and the others stopped meeting, knowing it was foolish to risk their own freedom.

'Since then, I go for prayer to the Orthodox Church, but I see before me the red, yellow and blue flag of the Army,' said Vera wistfully. For her, the freedom claimed by the State was not real. She could not talk to anyone, even relatives, about what was most important in her life.

Quietly asking her new friend to pray for her, Vera slipped away – a frail, grey figure – across the dusty ground until she was lost among the crowds of other grey people.

On return to Sweden the visitor followed the urge to write to *Stridsropet*, the Swedish *War Cry*, telling of her encounter and asking readers to pray for people like Vera, who were deprived of so much which others take for granted.

There were many faithful Christians like Vera, but younger generations, largely satisfied physically and mentally, did not perceive the need to develop a third, spiritual, dimension. Patriotic parades and anthems replaced the yearning in Russian souls for something to revere.

Thus throughout these years of the cold war a thin red, yellow and blue thread, spun with printed word and inspired lives, remained though stretched almost to breaking point. And still Salvationists around the world prayed for the people of Russia and donated money in faith that one day the Army would return.

In 1954, the time of Khrushchev's brief thaw in the cold war, Alexander Karev, General Secretary of the Russian Baptist Church, was able to travel to Sweden. In an interview published in the Swedish *War Cry* he told how he had attended Army meetings in Petrograd 37 years previously. His interest had been stirred by reading a copy of *Vestnik Spasseniya*. Declaring that he wanted to be a warrior of the Lord, as well as a member of a church community, he recounted one of Karl Larsson's sermons which had made an impression on him at the beginning of his Christian pilgrimage. Alexander patterned his own ministry on the Army's methods, having observed how effective they were. Army leaders became friends and mentors from whom he had learnt the secret of caring for the whole person, soul and body.

His radiant face as he sang Army songs in a Stockholm meeting was an inspiration to Salvationists who had prayed for so long that the word of God would not be void in Russia. Here was living proof of the power of the Holy Spirit.

The only regret when they were told that a number of former Salvationists now belonged to the Baptist Church, which was legally recognised at the time, was that Commissioner Karl Larsson was not alive to hear the news. But as he was in Heaven, he already knew it! He had once resolved that when he got there the first thing he would do was look for his Russian friends.

A retirement journey back to his roots in Sweden led American Salvation Army officer, Lieutenant-Colonel Henry Rostett, to explore further and go to Moscow. He discovered that the first coach tour to be granted permission to enter Russia was about to leave – and there were two vacancies on board. What's more, the organisers wanted a person to take responsibility for morning prayers on the journey and Henry fitted the bill.

On the first morning he warily watched the reactions of the Russian guide as he stood at the front of the coach, Bible in hand, and led a short act of worship. He need not have worried. The guide showed respect for the practice and interest in the new ideas to which he was exposed.

It was possible for the tourists to join a congregation of Baptists worshipping in their Moscow church. Henry was proud to tell the pastor of his Salvationist heritage, and even more pleased to discover that the Founder's song, 'O boundless salvation', was enjoyed by Baptists in Russia and that the biography of William Booth, who was recognised as a social reformer, was to be found in Soviet libraries.

Bandsman Bernard Platt, from Rochdale, England, visited the USSR in the early 1960s at a time which was especially significant for Russian Christians. The government publishing house had just issued 20,000 copies of the Bible, the first officially published for 40 years. This was small compensation for the thousands of Christian books which had been confiscated and destroyed in the days of hard-line Communism but it was at least a recognition that the Scriptures were valid. Once again Khrushchev's regime had allowed a breath of warm air to waft through the country.

In spite of this gesture, churches were still short of Bibles. Many of the new issue went straight to public libraries where they would be seen more as examples of foreign classical literature than as a guide to life. Bernard Platt saw people hungry for the printed word in a large Baptist church. Half the sizeable congregation, which included a few young people among the elderly, gladly stood throughout the long service. They sang sincerely from hand-copied hymnbooks.

At this time, the Baptist Church, some half-a-million strong, rented state-owned property, and was forbidden to teach children at separate sessions. This situation was accepted readily by those who remembered far greater restrictions.

Bernard Platt was warmly received, especially by a pastor who had once attended a Salvation Army meeting in London and been inspired by the preaching of the then Commissioner Frederick Coutts.

Young people in Russia were not often willing to be associated with formal religion and what they were led to believe were superstitious or simple-minded practices. They were more likely to take notice of *Konsomolskaya Pravda*, the journal of the Communist youth movement with a circulation of seven million.

In 1969, one of the paper's correspondents was sent to Sweden to investigate the moral state of Swedish youth, aiming to demonstrate the superiority of the Russian ethos. During his investigations at one of Stockholm's notorious nightspots the reporter was impressed by the sight of a Salvationist helping a drunken man to his home. Visible drunkenness was not countenanced in his country and those who were found helpless in the streets were dealt with abruptly, if not brutally. This was a new approach. He wanted to know more.

Arrangements were made for him to visit Headquarters in Stockholm where the Chief Secretary, Colonel Harry Tyndal, took time to explain Salvation Army principles relating to moral issues. He went on to tell the reporter about Army work among victims of abuse and neglect, pointing out that many years previously Russian Salvationists had been involved in similar ministry.

Thoughtfully and honestly the reporter filed his copy. Yes, there was decadence in the West but there were also those who cared enough to show compassion to its victims. Millions of young Russians read the article, the vast majority becoming conscious of The Salvation Army and its social involvement for the first time.

Another incidence of Russian interest in The Salvation Army had an unusual setting. Captain and Mrs Len McNeilly, New Zealand officers, were sailing on a Russian passenger liner from France to Canada. A Methodist fellow-passenger suggested that they might lead a Christian Sunday service on board, and asked the captain for permission. This was acceptable, providing the service was not announced over the ship's tannoy.

Anxious to use the opportunity well, they set about writing 100 invitations which they offered to people at Sunday breakfast. Co-opting the dance pianist, they arranged chairs in the White Nights saloon ready for the congregation. Perhaps only a few would come. After all, Christians were frowned on in Russia. But faith was rewarded, and the lounge was filled with 70 people listening to the gospel message. The good news was reported in the New Zealand *War Cry* dated 21 April 1973.

A Salvation Army ambassador to Russia who travelled there several times before and after perestroika was Mrs Colonel Violet Williams. Opportunity came in connection with her responsibilities in the Women's World Day of Prayer organisation. She made her second visit in 1982. A congregation of more than a thousand people heard her preach in the Moscow Central Baptist Church before lifting their voices in the triumphant hymn 'All hail the power of Jesus' name' as the service concluded. By contrast, at the invitation of the British Ambassador, Sir Charles Keeble, she attended an intimate Anglican service at the embassy chapel.

In conversation with Mrs Williams, the secretary of women's work in the Russian Baptist Church revealed that her parents had been converted at the Army in Petrograd years before and been enrolled as soldiers. The young Salvationist who had called at their house and linked them with the corps became a Baptist minister when the Army was proscribed, and they joined him at his church. Now their daughter was continuing the line of service, in spite of many hindrances over the years.

Mrs Williams went to Moscow again in 1989. As well as visiting her Baptist friends she was taken to a new 1,000-bed children's hospital. Some of the wards were full of badly-injured children, swathed in bandages, victims of the recent Armenian earthquake disaster. Catching their smiles as she bent over to comfort them, Mrs Williams determined to do what she could to help. Her doctor son had sophisticated equipment to back up his expertise. This hospital, modern as it was, had very little equipment. Dressings and drugs were carefully rationed. Skilled doctors and dedicated nurses were constantly hampered in their work by lack of resources.

Mrs Williams had friends in high places back in England! She asked for an appointment with Queen Elizabeth, the Queen Mother, to talk about her experiences. They had met a number of times in connection with the Women's World Day of Prayer movement, and they relaxed as they drank morning tea together. The plight of the children moved the Queen Mother. 'We must do something. They deserve all the help we can give them,' she said.

So it was that two determined women made a difference to staff and patients in a hospital far away. With the Queen Mother's

15

generous gift, Mrs Williams, advised by her son, purchased needles, syringes, water-beds, bandages, drip-feeds and other specialised equipment unobtainable in the USSR, and personally presented them to delighted staff back in Moscow.

A less tangible yet effective gift of music had been taken to Christians in Leningrad in 1985. Two bus-loads of Salvationists and friends from Finland and Sweden crossed the Russian border on one of the regular holiday tours arranged by the Army. The bandsmen among them packed their brass instruments and Army uniforms ready to proclaim the gospel in the universal language of music. They seized the opportunity to play to more than a thousand people gathered in the Baptist church for worship. Although Army music festivals are commonplace in the West, this was no ordinary event. It was another link in the chain of recognition.

No less a person than the Soviet Ambassador to Sweden, Boris Pankin, later prophesied the Army's return to his country when he was presented with a cheque for Armenian relief by Commissioner Anna Hannevik, the Territorial Commander, at Sweden's 1989 congress. 'I read about the Army as a child, and knew it had a mission of mercy,' he told the crowd of Salvationists in congress. 'Charity is finding its way back. Maybe one day we'll see The Salvation Army back in the Soviet Union.'

Many hearing these words, and reading them in the next day's press, were sceptical. This would not happen for years – if ever. Even those reading the front page report of the event in the UK *Salvationist* of 22 July would have found it hard to believe that just two years later the ambassador's speculations would be proved accurate.

All these contacts encouraged those who heard of them. The work of the early days had not been in vain. Although the Army's influence seemed minuscule in such a vast union of nations, God has a wonderful way of increasing that which is offered in his name. There was a hope that one day . . . perhaps . . . the doors would open wide again enabling Salvation Army soldiers to march in the streets of Russian towns and villages, and to care for people desperately in need of compassion. For some, who felt a strong empathy with those who had been deprived of religious freedom for so long, it was more than a hope; it was a belief. It would happen in God's time, and they would be ready.

Chapter 3

FINDING THE KEY

Would glasnost open the door?

SALVATIONISTS and other Christians were ready to return to Russia. The question was, when would Russia be ready to unlock the door and welcome them? The legacy of Lenin's deep hatred of Christianity had evolved into ignorance and apathy towards the Church. Who needed Heaven when they were citizens of the perfect earthly State?

But by this time there were many, both inside and outside the USSR, who knew that the monolith was far from perfect and some even dared to say so. Rapidly-changing technology and communications enabled the world to see over the top of the wall of secrecy. It was like looking back in time. The lives of the people seemed to be set in dull grey concrete. Even provision for culture and relaxation was fixed in a rigid mould. Literature, theatre, music and television reflected only the same monochrome.

Technical progress, involving high spending, was devoted to the military machine, not to improving the comfort and convenience of people's everyday lives. Citizens were crowded into faceless apartment blocks. Thousands of country folk still drew water from wells and milked goats tethered on the roadside. And the grey, shadowy but real, KGB made sure that it stayed that way.

Khrushchev, unlike his predecessors, travelled the world. It was different out there. Perhaps it wasn't all bad. Maybe it was time to change. But the big-power, sabre-rattling game had some rounds to go. Czechoslovakia, Cuba, Hungary, Afghanistan, convinced Communists to close ranks again. Like a proud old woman with her own ideas, Mother Russia was self-sufficient.

Still, proud old people in the natural course of things grow weaker and need help, and wise ones accept it. The catalyst of change was Chernobyl. In 1986 the compassionate, shocked response of people outside the Eastern bloc to the nuclear disaster was wisely and gratefully accepted. Perhaps there were strings attached, and scarcely-veiled criticism, but the need was too urgent to stop to think about it. There really were friends out there.

Mikhail Gorbachev, General Secretary of the Communist Party of the Soviet Union since the previous year, committed to change, stretched out his hand to the West. Instead of the closed fist his predecessors had raised, his hand was open in friendship – and in supplication. His privileged position gave him access to the truth about the dire economic state of the nation. He needed help, and this meant openness – glasnost. That word, with its fellow, perestroika – restructuring – became the new Soviet slogan. Those abroad who had been taken in for years by Soviet propaganda were shocked. Their strong foe needed help. Was it a Trojan-horse trick? What would happen to those who entered the open door in good faith?

The Salvation Army was ready to take risks. It was obvious to everyone that practical help was needed, but Christians were also aware of the spiritual poverty which had been forced on the Soviet people. The call, 'Come over and help us!' could not be ignored. In Army tradition, physical and spiritual nourishment would be offered as a complete package. It was a combination many still in authority in Russia found it hard to accept. Countries just across Russian borders – Norway, Sweden, Finland, Denmark, Korea – where The Salvation Army flourished, had strong emotional, almost tribal, links with their huge neighbour. Their people had been its pioneers at the beginning of the century. They were to be pioneers again.

One of the 'new' ideas filtering into Russia was the concept of charity. Until now, those dealing with problem people, seen as society's failures, did so as an unpleasant duty. They had been ordered to sweep the dirt under the carpet. One had a responsibility towards one's family and the State – no more. Of course, there were many whose spirit was not frozen, giving help where they saw need around them, but they were not respected. It was not the Soviet way to be compassionate. The Christian grace of prayer was unknown to many and scorned by others, but where it was sincerely introduced to them its significance was acknowledged.

Commissioner Anna Hannevik, leader of the Army in Sweden, was invited to the Soviet Embassy in Stockholm in 1990 to receive on behalf of the Army recognition of help given to victims of the Armenian earthquake. Publicly, Minister Vassilijev recalled a previous visit. 'Commissioner Hannevik has been here before, and that occasion was the very first time I consciously prayed as she worshipped God with me,' he confessed adding, significantly, 'We need The Salvation Army and hope you will soon come to Russia – and create a division with a Russian commissioner.'

Now in this new spring, when even government ministers spoke openly about prayer, those who cared about others were not afraid, and a group of such people organised The Leningrad Charity Society. Looking for support from like-minded groups, they contacted The Salvation Army and Commissioner Ingrid Lindberg, in command of the Army in Finland, eagerly responded.

In January 1990, accompanied by Captain Tarja Suominen, Ingrid Lindberg joined a tourist group, travelling the route so often journeyed by Karl Larsson more than 70 years previously. The Charity Society had arranged a two-day programme for them. A Finnish Salvationist medical student, Sari Pekkerinen, was to be their translator. What they heard and saw seemed very familiar. It was just like visiting the social and community programme of an active Salvation Army corps. The schedule included practical help for needy people in their homes, prison and hospital visits, children's clubs, therapy for bruised and aching limbs. This, of course, was not done in a Christian context, although some of the people involved were believers. With a core of professional people and a training course for 21 student social workers the society was surging forward.

At the society's headquarters in the centre of Leningrad the Salvationists had a strong sense of déjà vu. There was a Salvation Army exhibition! This confirmed the rightness of going into Russia. In God's economy it was sensible to use a successful strategy again.

To discover how a Salvation Army exhibition came to be in Leningrad we must trace another thread in the saga, this time leading back to Canada. Dr Ross Wilcock, a Salvationist from Woodstock, Ontario, was not only a pathologist with a wide range of scientific and social interests but also an avid reader of Tolstoy's works. He was fascinated particularly by the religious writings of the great Russian author. So often his ideas ran parallel to those of Salvation Army thinkers. If ever Russia's door was open again to Christian faith, Ross felt sure that the Army could play an important role.

Attending a conference on the prevention of nuclear warfare in June 1988, Ross discovered fellow Tolstoyians among the Russian delegates. They agreed they must keep in touch. So it was that in November Ross visited his new friends in Leningrad. Naturally, they talked of Tolstoy and that which he seemed to have in common with William and Catherine Booth.

In 1878, at the same time as The Christian Mission was evolving into The Salvation Army, Tolstoy in Russia had finally rejected Orthodoxy and was searching for an alternative creed. The following year, he began writing *What I Believe*, one of the books which was later to impact on Ross's thinking. Ross and his

Russian friends, citizens of two vastly different cultures, were excited to discover that deep in their psyche they had common spiritual roots. The Salvationist believed passionately that the Army's practical, Spirit-motivated approach was right for a desolate nation. His friends wanted to pursue the idea. Knowing that history, as well as Tolstoy, is high on the scale of interest in Leningrad, it was decided that an exhibition would be an attractive way of informing people about this international church which had been a small part of their past.

Display material from the Army in Canada and International Headquarters was attractively arranged with Russian captions. An Army uniform and flag from Finland ensured that, when the Army did march again in Leningrad, a time which the historian in charge of the exhibition dreamed of, some would recognise what it stood for. Ross journeyed to Leningrad again to stay for five weeks while the exhibition was open, keen to build on any interest shown. One young woman who was especially interested, Nadya Burova, was invited to spend time with Ross and Alison, his wife, to see something of Army life in Canada. She later wrote, 'Dr Ross Wilcock has had a profound effect on my life. My impressions of The Salvation Army had previously come from literature where they're often portrayed as caricatures in a mocking fashion. Now I see that your goals are pure – to be kind. This is something we need urgently and what is good about it is that you have developed a structure so your mechanism works smoothly. We need to borrow from The Salvation Army's spiritual attitudes and your mechanism for dispensing kindness.'

Nadya and about 20 intellectual friends had formed a new group, The Centre for Creative Initiatives for Peace, and they were excited by the way in which this particular initiative was taking shape. Plans were proposed for a group from Toronto to visit Russia in the late spring to explore further ways in which The Salvation Army could become involved in the USSR. Nadya would be a key figure in this expedition. Good press coverage of the exhibition was also encouraging. 'An army without weapons!' declared one headline in a Leningrad evening paper. The article went on to describe the Army's charity work in many parts of the world.

This information would strike a chord with those Russians who, like Ross Wilcock's friends, in the course of travel abroad had seen the Army at work. Others who had been less privileged but who had an insatiable appetite for new things flooding into the country were interested to discover more about this unusual army. Film – an important part of Russia's media – was also used to bring Army scenes, including its ministry to homeless and neglected people in the West, into the homes of Russian people. Quite a few echoed the opinion heard one evening in a Moscow news report: 'What is needed here is The Salvation Army.'

After appraising the exhibition, Commissioner Lindberg had long discussions with several influential people including the chairman of the society, Mr A. D. Granin, who was a member of the praesidium in Moscow. The Russians respected the expertise and experience the Army showed in social work and were keen to learn this. She prayed that they would learn too the spiritual springs of service given in the name of Jesus, as she later explained the Army's doctrine as well as its methods during a two-hour lecture to members of the society. As they were about to return home Commissioner Lindberg and her fellow Salvationists were happily surprised when a suitcase full of new toys they had brought for children in hospital was returned to them – not empty, but packed with Russian toys to take back for Finnish children. So often Russian generosity is buried under a mountain of incoming aid, but not in this instance!

Commissioner Lindberg was disappointed that contacts with Metropolitan Alexi of the Orthodox Church had not resulted in a meeting, although she later received a warm letter from him. She did, however, enjoy part of a Baptist service and a friendly talk with the pastor, who had been allowed freedom to hold open-air meetings in the centre of Leningrad.

Returning on the train, Commissioner Lindberg and Captain Suominen had plenty to discuss about how to build on this opening. It would be a two-way process: Russian children could go to Finland for camp holidays and older young people go to study social work, while Finnish students and professionals could spend time helping members of the Leningrad Charity Society in their expanding work. Videos and music cassettes could be exchanged.

'We must not wait, now the doors are open. The Army has the message that the people's hearts are crying for,' wrote Commissioner Lindberg in her report to International Headquarters. It happened – though not as quickly as she would have liked! There were others who were more cautious about taking this enormous step of faith, not to mention thousands of forms to be filled in and official seals to be earned.

The exhibition was still a focus of interest in May when Salvationists Fiona and Stephen Hill made the long journey to Leningrad from Horsham, Australia. They were impressed by what they saw of community work in action – counselling, therapy for handicapped children and practical help for the elderly – run by the Leningrad Charitable Society. Many facts and ideas were exchanged. One of the members offered a practical contact for the time when the Army came back to Russia. He knew a fine tailor in Moscow who would make good uniforms!

At International Headquarters, keen observers of the situation realised that glasnost must surely be the key to reopening the door into Leningrad and Moscow. Already neighbouring territories had been asked to make links with emerging states – Switzerland with Hungary, The Netherlands with Czechoslovakia, Sweden with Latvia, Finland with Estonia and the German Territory with Eastern Germany.

Norwegian Salvationists were delegated to build on the goodwill they had established with Russia both in Leningrad and in the far northern town of Murmansk, where Major Gilbert Ellis and Norwegian and Finnish Salvationists had made a number of visits.

Known worldwide for its generosity, Norway had contributed more than a million kroner through The Salvation Army to victims of the Armenian earthquake. Now they wanted to help in any way they could. The Territorial Commander of Norway, Iceland and The Faroes Territory, Commissioner Einar Madsen, and his staff took hold of the responsibility willingly and with awe. At the first committee meeting on 8 March 1990 plans were formulated. The group was to discover, like everyone else involved in the perestroika process, that plans and reality were often poles apart.

It was wise to make approaches through official channels and in this case staff at the Soviet Embassy in Oslo were most helpful. A meeting was convened at the end of March with representatives of various bodies responsible for religious affairs in Russia. Some pertinent questions were cautiously asked. It was not so long ago that the main responsibility of Russian officials towards religion was to repress it. It was important to see things clearly or the whole exciting project could prove abortive. How would the authorities view requests to reopen Salvation Army work in Russia? If they consented, what help could best be given?

Answers established that if the Army operated within the framework of the law and caused no violence it would be welcome to distribute literature and food. The fact that frequent changes in the law made that framework rather unstable might have occurred to those on both sides of the table! In the light of this meeting a detailed request to begin a Salvation Army programme in Russia was prepared. The following month Yuri Petrenko, a Soviet diplomat in Oslo, promised to translate and forward the letter with a current copy of *The Salvation Army Year Book* to the Religious Committee of the USSR in Moscow. There were also medical and educational committees as well as specific churches who had appealed for help. These might well provide other lines of possible approach.

One such approach followed up by the Army in Ottawa led to an exchange of Canadian and Soviet social workers interested in alcohol rehabilitation programmes. It was likely that such work could be undertaken by the Army in Russia, but it was important to make it clear from the beginning that the Army's priority was to preach the gospel. Under no other pretext could it enter the country and expect God to prosper the work. It was hard for some people in the medical field, desperately short of both specialised equipment and simple consumable stock, to understand why a philanthropic international group was unable to promise substantial additions to the amount of help they had already given to a number of hospitals. This proved a difficult quandary more than once, and could never really be resolved. Similar dilemmas were to arise with regard to teaching in schools and institutes but this was more easily dealt with as time could be given where large sums of money could not.

Within a month a reply to the request for a permit was delivered personally by Petrenko. Clarification was needed on some points. Would Russian nationals be actively involved in the Army's ministry or would it be run entirely by foreigners? This matter needed serious consideration, but at least the approach had not been rejected. In Petrenko's opinion, the financial help the Army had already given, and more schemes which were planned, would count in favour of the Movement's acceptance. That summer Norwegian Salvationists were to play host to a number of children from Chernobyl. Clear mountain air would be a tonic for these youngsters from a severely-polluted region. They would also benefit from the warmth of the families into which they would be welcomed. It was another positive link recognised by the embassy.

Petrenko and his colleague, First Secretary Vladimir Kalugin, respected the Army and they were happy to facilitate early official visits to their country. All this was reported to General Eva Burrows in London. She was thrilled with opportunities which were opening faster than anyone had dreamt possible. Could it be that she would lead the Army into Russia before her term of office ended? Carefully the information was studied at a meeting the General convened in May. Commissioner Caughey Gauntlett had been called out of retirement to co-ordinate the Army's movement eastwards. His experience as a child in Eastern Europe gave him some insight into his responsible task and he listened with keen interest to reports on each area of proposed expansion.

Balancing positive with negative, it was agreed that the moves should go ahead, financed by International Headquarters together with help already offered for specific projects by the United States of America. A straightforward approach to the most senior officials was recommended rather than trying other links which might prove successful in the short-term but could have serious repercussions. There were already so many strands of activity – Norway, Sweden, USA, Canada, Australia, Finland – which must be bound into a strong cord of united action. They could so easily become a tangled web which would hinder development.

With such swift progress it was essential to seek out suitable personnel. There were not too many Russian-speaking, adaptable people with a fearless, energetic commitment to God and the Army around, but God had his servants in mind and had been preparing them for many years. Now the call went out.

One who was ready for the call was Sandra Ryan, a cadet in Canada at this time. Nadya Burova (of the Centre for Creative Initiatives for Peace) had completed her plans for a group to visit from Toronto, and Sandra had been selected as one of the seven members of the delegation. Led by Lieut-Colonel Bruce Halsey, the group visited Leningrad, Moscow and Kiev in a whirlwind of activity and returned home with a kaleidoscope of memories and impressions: blind children responding to choruses about Jesus . . . the spiritual strength of the Russian people, like a deep well within them . . . the struggle in hospitals and other institutions to cope with old-fashioned equipment and outdated methods . . . the glistening eyes of a tourist guide as she listened to the group singing 'O boundless salvation' in a small museum inside the Kremlin which had been the private chapel of patriarchs . . . the enthusiastic response to the Army open-air meeting outside

Moscow's McDonald's . . . the eagerness with which so many accepted copies of the Bible.

Returning breathlessly to Toronto to recount it all, the team felt as if they had been away for a year! They reported that, from this evidence, Russians were ready to be introduced to a compassionate, spiritual movement like The Salvation Army and then commit themselves to service in its ranks.

It was imperative to discover as much as possible from every angle about the current temperature in Russia, especially in respect of religion. A new law on religious freedom revising the draconian version introduced by Stalin in 1929 was being carved out by politicians during that spring and summer. Dr Garfield Williams, a churchman with wide ecumenical contacts in Eastern Europe, did much to pave the way for the Army. It was hoped that cordial relationships could be established with the Orthodox Church which had stood for almost a thousand years at the centre of Russia's faith and thinking. The Army has proved again and again that it is possible to work side-by-side with other Christian denominations, and Salvationists were anxious not to displace but to complement those who had kept the faith through dark times.

This was a period of particular uncertainty in the Orthodox Church as Patriarch Pimen had died after a long illness and his successor had yet to be chosen. Garfield Williams pointed out that the election of the new patriarch, to be held that June, was crucial as far as relationships with the Army were concerned.

In fact Metropolitan Alexi was elected and took his place in the centre of the political, as well as church, arena. This dual role pleased some, but disappointed radical Christians who hoped that the Orthodox Church would learn to speak with an independent voice. His election coincided with that of Yeltsin to the chair of the Russian Parliament.

The two protagonists represented powerful establishments, both striving for a new identity after years in the wilderness. What effect would these giants have on emerging groups like The Salvation

Army? Garfield Williams had taken an opportunity to speak about the Army to Alexi, who had personally invited him to attend a highly-significant occasion – his first celebration of the liturgy as patriarch in St Isaac's Cathedral, which for 62 years had been only a museum. At the same event Williams was introduced to the new President, Boris Yeltsin. He knew that these brief contacts could be most important in the ecumenical field and he generously recommended The Salvation Army to the new patriarch who expressed a hope that he could meet representatives of the Army if they let him know when they expected to be in Moscow.

In the light of these conversations and contacts, Garfield Williams told Army leaders that the situation was promising and advised that careful timing of the first move into the country was crucial.

These were sensitive times. Although the 'head' of the great nation wanted to move on towards the 21st century, the heavy hindquarters of the Russian bear were dragging. Newfangled ideas, criticism of all they had built their hopes on, the intrusions of loudmouthed foreigners, were all too much. It was painful to acknowledge the failure of the old system, especially for those who still had vested interests in it. The Salvation Army is an international organisation by conviction but it is made up of individuals whose national background has formed their character and outlook. How could they convince members of this proud nation – officials, students, workers, intellectuals – that they could work together across boundaries to build the universal Kingdom of God? Only by the grace of God can such things be achieved. The continuing story is proof.

Chapter 4

TURNING THE KEY

Stronger links are forged

COMMISSIONER Caughey Gauntlett's first visit to Russia took place in September 1990. Accompanying a lorry-load of food, toys, Bibles and information brochures, he set out from Oslo to Leningrad via Sweden and Finland with five officers and their Salvationist translator, Minna Karlström.

Minna, a 22-year-old Finn, was to play a key role in establishing the Army in Russia/CIS. In the course of her study to become a qualified interpreter in Russian, she recognised that religious vocabulary had been expunged from the Russian language. Archaic words were known by some but plausible modern terms to describe spiritual experiences and ideas didn't exist. Minna set about preparing a vocabulary which would 'make the message clear and plain' in contemporary Russia. She also made a collection of hymns sung by Salvationists early in the century and some from the current Baptist repertoire. These would be valuable for Russian-speaking groups outside the country as well as future Salvationists in Russia. Expatriate Salvationists were to value highly the skill and support of translators who, like Minna, would give them a voice and understanding in their early days of ministry.

A good translator is indispensable when it comes to dealing with customs officials, too! From Stockholm, the party took an overnight ferry to Helsinki then, after greeting Finnish officers, went on to the border. Nervously they waited for an hour while Minna negotiated complex formalities, and then proceeded on their mission.

Although the Communist Party was still officially in control of the USSR, glasnost had encouraged people with shared interests outside the Communist ethos to meet together. These informal groups drew together those who enjoyed sport, computer games, rock music, in an atmosphere which was far more relaxed than the centrally-organised Communist activities which were all they had known.

Some of these groups comprised those who wanted to bring about improvements in their society and to make links with the rest of the world. Naturally they included experienced people who had been active for years in the Communist structure of local government but whose ideas were gradually changing as a result of perestroika.

Other philanthropic movements came from a different stable, giving people who had been marginalised – if not actually exiled – opportunity to introduce openly ideas previously regarded as beyond the pale. The Leningrad Charitable Society and the Centre for Creative Initiatives for Peace have already been mentioned.

The Army in Norway had made links with the Leningrad branch of the Friendship Society which was responsible to the government for arranging official visits. Andrey T. Ibragimov, vice-chairman of the society, who helped the Army party considerably, later became involved in business and formed the first Rotary Club in Russia. The Children's Fund, a group which was trying to raise the standard of care for sick and disabled children, arranged for Salvationists to visit hospitals and special schools distributing gifts they had brought in by lorry.

Many discussions were held in the relaxed fashion typical of Russian protocol where people scrutinise each other, while making polite conversation round the samovar. The Army's Christian motivation, as well as its social aims, was made clear in every case, whether it was a church, social or State connection.

Talks were interspersed with visits to institutions caring professionally for hundreds of children. Gifts were given and appreciated, but even more valued was the fact that people outside the USSR were taking an interest in what the staff, some of whom were Christians, were trying to achieve. The isolation of former days had been painful. Any point of contact eased the pain while offers of practical help lightened the shameful burden of working with inadequate resources.

It was apparent in conversation with church leaders that the social conscience of both the Baptist and Orthodox Churches was being stirred. The State, which had regulated its people from cradle to grave, was delegating responsibilities it could no longer fulfil to those with the will and the resources to take them on. The Orthodox Church was about to open a small hospital in Leningrad. The Baptists, whose membership had more than doubled to 76 congregations since 1988, were looking for help as they tried to begin solving the community's great needs. They recognised the Army's expertise in this field but urged them to begin with open-air and door-to-door ministry when they received permission, as seemed likely, to work in the city.

Professor Boris B. Bondarenko, of the First Baptist Church of Leningrad, who had worshipped at a Salvation Army corps when he studied in Canada, was especially keen to help when the day came. Perhaps understandably, a number of church leaders hoped that the Army would work ecumenically, rather than revive a distinctive group. They were increasingly aware of groups, many of them with dubious leadership and little access to good Bible teaching, which were mushrooming in the fertile soil of glasnost.

As Commissioner Gauntlett and his colleagues surveyed the needs they could easily have been overwhelmed. Every hospital they visited was hopeful that the contact would lead to a source of supplies. In many instances it did. The need for care of the homeless and rehabilitation of people disabled by alcohol abuse, injury or disease was obvious in the city streets, day and night.

It was easy to disturb and disappoint the fragile morale of Russians involved in medicine, education and community housing who were doing their best to come to terms with the past and find a solution for the future. There were many ways in which The Salvation Army could serve, but incoming personnel would have to balance sensitivity with strength. Officials responsible for signing the necessary documents would only do so if they felt the Army's motives were in keeping with their vision for the nation. Practical things like property, bank accounts, telephone lines, all depended on those documents. In this respect it was no different from 1913. Would the answer be the same?

Returning to England, Commissioner Gauntlett spent five short weeks reporting on the visit and co-ordinating dates and methods of approach for the next journey which was to be to Moscow in October 1990. Before leaving London he was able to meet Nadya Burova and Ross Wilcock. He valued this opportunity to hear a first-hand account of the Canadian party's experiences in Russia and to establish realistic guidelines for any future co-operation between Nadya's society and the Army. So many appeals for help were coming from all directions that even an established international movement like The Salvation Army could not make promises to meet every need. The Army's proposed plan was to follow the development of 1913, opening first in Leningrad and then in Moscow.

The visit to Moscow involved many more discussions with officials as well as sightseeing and cultural events. Salvationist Dr John Coutts, a linguist with a keen interest in developments in the USSR, joined the party as interpreter.

Dealing with Russian law was rather like grappling with a wriggling eel. As fast as the finer points of a particular issue were grasped, the law changed, and the struggle began again. Religious

33

issues had been summarily dealt with in the past with little attempt to understand spiritual matters. Christian activity, unless strictly controlled and Orthodox, had been out of bounds. Now that the world had vested interests in the Soviet Union the issue of freedom of religion was a sensitive one.

On 1st October 1990 Gorbachev had signed the new law on religious freedom which had been under discussion for months. Now the required process would be clearer, if not easier. One thing stipulated by the new law was that each republic would have the responsibility of registering new churches in its own way. Even Leningrad and Moscow would require separate applications. It has been proved many times that patience, understanding and a sense of humour are required when dealing with matters of registration, whether it be for a Christian organisation or a vehicle, a congress or a holiday.

Caughey Gauntlett and his Norwegian colleagues, Commissioner Einar Madsen, Colonel Brynjar Welander, Lieut-Colonel John Bjartveit, Major Knut Ytterdahl and Captain Liv Guntvedt, grappled purposefully with each issue as they met officials of the Friendship Society, the Children's Foundation, the Baptist and Evangelical Union, the new Commission for Religious Affairs (the former council under another name), the External Relationships Committee of the Orthodox Church, the Soviet Foundation for Health and Charity, the Moscow Charitable Society. The last named was responsible for co-ordinating 90 community-based charitable organisations in Moscow alone!

Trying to balance all these views in the haven of their hotel on the last evening of the visit, the group agreed to recommend advancing with plans to open work in Russia. Perhaps the remark of one official as he accepted a Bible was the key: 'I have read all the books which criticise the Bible,' he said, handling the book, 'but I have never actually opened one.' That had to be the priority – to open God's word and reveal the Word made flesh. Only this would satisfy the spiritual hunger of those who recognised their need.

A report reaching the General's desk from Lieut-Colonel George Church confirmed this priority. The colonel, with Mr Gordon Bingham, had been a delegate at an international conference of charity organisations, sponsored by the Haaz Fund and held in the southern town of Odessa. This socially active charitable group, one of the first to be formed in the USSR, in 1987, worked in close co-operation with the Orthodox Church and had strong links in the United States. In calling the conference it was hoped to establish mutually-beneficial links between the USSR and the USA.

The Salvationist delegates had been gladly welcomed both by participants and the local press. Some who approached them were primarily interested in financial help but the majority saw that the Army could help to meet a different need. 'People are looking for something to believe in. The values of caring must be learned again,' said one speaker, expressing the hope that the Army would return to Russia.

After the conference George Church made contact with Boris Bondarenko, following up links made by the group from Canada four months previously. Here was more evidence that the Army would be welcomed to play a significant role in this time of change.

An exciting development was the plan for a 24-hour telethon, *St Petersburg: Renaissance*, which would take place in Leningrad on 6 January 1991, the Russian Orthodox Christmas Eve. The independent Russian TV company preparing the production was keen to feature the Army, filming in North America as well as in Scandinavia. Here was another valuable opportunity for good public relations.

A Russian journalist, Valentin Ostrovsky, mourned the loss of many positive human values which, as he wrote, had 'gone down the drain' in his country. Sensing that The Salvation Army upheld these values, he contacted the Army in London and arrangements were made for him to see many aspects of Christian involvement in the community. He travelled from Hoxton to Southampton,

Nottingham to Swindon, Bournemouth to Highworth, seeing not only effective programmes but discerning the motivating Spirit.

Things he saw and read made a deep impression. He found a keynote in the Army songbook and copied down the couplet:

In a world of shifting values
There are standards that remain.

(*No 324, The Song Book of The Salvation Army*)

Determined to do something to bring those values to light again, he returned to Moscow and wrote a comprehensive article for the new *Literary Gazette International*, which he edited. In the first issue, December 1990, the article appeared under the banner headline, 'Why we need The Salvation Army'.

The magazine targeted the intelligentsia, but the message of this article was clear to the simplest reader. Vivid word pictures of kindness in action among disadvantaged people in Britain prefaced an unambiguous closing statement: 'We need Salvationists right here, right now. They are more than welcome in our country. We need their strength of faith, their vigorous optimism and, most of all, we need their shining example that could trigger off a chain reaction of kindness in our troubled society.'

General Eva Burrows, ready to take up such challenges, was eager to move forward at the right moment. Two days after Commissioner Gauntlett returned to London a conference was held at IHQ. In addition to senior staff responsible for development in Europe, Lieut-Colonel Bruce Halsey, from Canada, was invited to attend. This was a significant event. A decision was made to move forward in God's name and by the power of his Spirit through the opening which had become apparent.

After deep discussion a number of practical recommendations were made. A pioneering group of five or six officers and soldiers would move into Leningrad the following spring with the aim of setting up a corps with a wide community outreach. For at least a year, the Norway Territory would continue responsibility for administration, following up the registration process and preparing a constitution. Lieut-Colonel Bjartveit was designated Officer-in-Charge and would keep IHQ informed of significant developments as they happened. Again the importance of clear lines of communication and respect for each player in the team was emphasised. So many people, both inside the USSR and in the Army world, were already waiting on the touchline, eager to see things happen. Fair play and skilled refereeing were essential in this vast field.

Soon news of the breathtaking plan hit the headlines in the Army press. For those who had prayed and believed for so long, it was the moment to praise God.

Chapter 5

THE DOOR UNLOCKS

Response to need opens the way

IN Oslo Commissioner Madsen watched the fax clicking out a lengthy letter. The venture was on! He was due to retire and would not be closely involved but he was thrilled to pass on the news that Norway's neighbourly interest was developing in a miraculous way. A small international team was being selected. John Bjartveit and his wife, responsible for work in the USSR from 1 January 1991, would be joined by Sven-Erik and Kathy Ljungholm, American captains currently serving in Sweden, and Sandra Ryan, with husband Geoff, now lieutenants, who would transfer to Leningrad just in time for the official opening.

This was planned for June or July, coinciding with a visit from the Oslo Temple Salvation Army Band. Minna Karlström, already experienced in working with Russian bureaucracy, would be with them for the summer.

With winter approaching, conditions for the poorest people in Leningrad were again difficult. Generous Norwegians provided clothes, food and medicines, which were transported to the city in conjunction with visits made to deal with registrations, property and other practical matters. Three tons were sent to Leningrad by lorry in November and six tons were taken in a trailer through to Moscow in December. Both consignments included Christmas gifts for children and staff in hospitals and other institutions where Salvationists had already made contact. Each visit revealed more shortages. A pioneering hospice for cancer patients urgently needed to replace old, uncomfortable beds. Through media publicity, a Norwegian hospital donated just what was needed. Bibles, including an attractively-illustrated children's Bible story book, were eagerly received.

The joy of giving was often dulled by an awareness that so many were still without. Pensioners on a small fixed income, disabled people – many of them amputees – orphans, large families, and an increasing number affected by the Aids virus were suffering in spite of the efforts of dozens of informal charitable groups working to obtain resources and use them to the best effect. At times attempts to build a structure within which to form a viable Army organisation were equally disheartening. The Mayor of Leningrad, Anatoly Sobchak, was courteous and encouraging, understanding the Army's desire to be registered as a church and not just a charitable organisation. But those minor officials who held the key to suitable properties, the seal to stamp a permit, or knowledge which would ease the process of obtaining legal status, were often confused, inefficient, or uncooperative. Naturally, in such circumstances, there were also those who were corrupt and saw the new freedoms as a means to private gain. It was difficult to know who to trust.

Visits made by Lieut-Colonel Bjartveit and his colleagues at the end of 1990 were helpful in strengthening links and gaining respect but disappointing as far as settling property, registration or financial matters were concerned. Coming from a country where efficiency and goodwill were commonplace it was hard to understand the motives and methods which they encountered.

But the overwhelming feeling towards the people of the USSR as Christmas approached that year was of friendship and compassion. Attitudes of suspicion, even hatred, which had begun to soften with the Moscow Olympic Games in 1980 and were further melted by the tragedies of Chernobyl and Armenia had been finally swept away with the Berlin Wall and the Iron Curtain.

New Year 1991 was a significant time for the city of Leningrad – soon to be called St Petersburg once again – and for The Salvation Army which hoped to be part of its restructuring. A Russia Office was established in Norway's THQ so that Lieut-Colonel Bjartveit and his wife could concentrate their efforts on preparations for the Army to re-enter Russia. The telethon *St Petersburg: Renaissance* was all set to go on 6 January. Commissioner and Mrs John Ord, the new territorial leaders in Norway, and Lieut-Colonel and Mrs Bjartveit flew to Leningrad as guests of Neva Television, excited by this opportunity to share in such a high-profile occasion. Dr Boris Bondarenko, Nikolai Grikurov, a soldier of Moss Corps in Norway, home for the winter holiday, Salvationists Dr and Mrs Ross Wilcox from Canada, and Russell Prince and Beverly Ventriss from the United States joined the group.

Presented live from the Kirov Theatre, the show was a tremendous international ecumenical occasion aimed at bringing hope to the dispirited city which had once been a glittering focus for the whole of Europe. Three hundred stars from the Soviet Union and abroad entertained the nationwide audience after a solemn opening marking the Christian Christmas festival led by members of the Orthodox and Armenian churches. The event was a focus on individuals and organisations who had offered practical help to restore the city's buildings, culture and spirituality. Five minutes of each hour were allocated to present the donors and to learn about their aims. Seizing this opportunity – which for them came at one o'clock in the morning – the Salvationists spoke to the cameras about the prime aims of The Salvation Army, backed up with film footage of compassionate action taken in Leningrad, Canada and the USA. Like a stone tossed into a quiet pool, the words and images transmitted in those five short minutes caused ripples of awareness far beyond the walls of the Kirov Theatre.

Later in the show, after the group had sung a gentle carol, every child in the audience was given a toy from an enormous Santa's sack of 750 toys sent by Canadian Salvationists. The others were distributed to children in orphanages and hospitals. From the States had come costly medicine which had been requested by a cancer research centre.

By the end of the event people's reactions indicated that they were open-minded to the Army. This was encouraging but if the Army was to remain in the city permanently, an open door into suitable premises was needed. The State had control of all property. One or two ideal premises had been viewed but vested interests were pulling in all directions. A foreign Christian organisation did not have much power on this playing field. Leaving a delegated lawyer and architect to wrestle with bureaucracy, the officers returned to Oslo.

Considerable progress in Estonia and Latvia, as well as the position in Russia, were reported at an international consultation in Oslo that February. Now it was time to work out more details. Lieut-Colonel Bjartveit proposed that the first priority was to establish a corps which should be firmly rooted in the community. It was estimated that a million people in the city, mostly elderly women, were undernourished. As before, attempts would be made to meet the physical needs of as many of these people as possible. Spiritual food was also a great need. Bibles were available in the Slavic language. The New Testament had been translated into modern Russian so young Russians would be encouraged to learn as they taught their younger brothers and sisters. Salvation Army teaching must be translated so that recruits would have a clear understanding of what being a Salvation Army soldier implied in both doctrinal and practical terms before they committed themselves to signing articles of war and wearing uniform. Deep religious traditions, such as the blessing of sacraments, had survived years of persecution and neglect and the Army's position must be sensitively understood.

In great faith, discussion went even beyond soldiership. A shortened training course, with continuing education, was thought to be appropriate for the first cadets who would be carefully nurtured for service in Russia and other Soviet countries. Always present was a subconscious awareness that the door might not be open to expatriate officers for long.

A date was set for the official reopening of The Salvation Army in Russia – 5 July 1991, when Oslo Temple Band was due to visit St Petersburg. An officer-couple would be posted into the city as soon as possible and the business of registration would be vigorously pursued.

Professional Russians, especially in medical and educational fields, were eager to grasp hold of opportunities to learn from the experience of others outside the Soviet Union and exchange visits continued. Doctors from the Leningrad Scientific Research Institute of Prosthetics benefited from a week's study of orthopaedics at the Norwegian National Hospital; two women studied methods of childcare in Norwegian Army centres; a delegation from the Centre of Creative Initiatives for Peace spent two weeks in Canada on a whirlwind tour of Salvation Army social centres and corps. Who can estimate the value of such experiences?

Readers of the UK Territory's *Salvationist* were given inspiring glimpses of life in the Soviet Union when Commissioner Caughey Gauntlett and Dr John Coutts recounted incidents from their visit to Russia in February 1991. They had taken every opportunity to distribute Christian literature in government offices, in children's homes, in hospitals and in Red Square itself.

'There is a great seeking, the outcome of spiritual hunger. Many have no idea of what they are looking for but sense there must be a meaning to life. And because "man cannot live by bread alone", they are trying to find some clue to that non-material "something" which is true life,' wrote Commissioner Gauntlett. A number of people, including the matron of a State children's home in Leningrad, openly witnessed to their Christian faith. 'What these children need is to learn about God, and to be led to accept Jesus Christ as their personal saviour,' she said.

John Coutts, whose experience of Soviet Russia is considerable, was fascinated by the juxtaposition of hardline methods and the new ideas to which they were gradually and reluctantly giving way. This process was symbolised by a forlorn statue of Marx, banished to the garden of the Council for Religious Affairs premises, and a great portrait of Lenin looking down on those who were rejecting the way of life he imposed. How would The Salvation Army fit into this constantly shifting society without being crushed between clashing factions? It was important to make the right approach.

Comprehensive reports of visits to St Petersburg and Moscow made by Lieut-Colonel Bjartveit and others during the following months illustrate the enormous frustrations of obtaining two important things – a constitution giving the Army a legal right to work in Russia, and property in which to base such work. Captain Peter Smith, IHQ's Legal and Parliamentary Secretary, travelled to St Petersburg to advise on the agreement being established between the city authorities and the Army, and to finalise the important constitution document to be signed by the General before being submitted to the Russian authorities for registration.

When such documents are prepared in two languages it is especially vital to ensure that there are no misleading clauses. It is also important to notice if anything vital has been omitted! Many Russians in control, seeing the Army as a wealthy Western organisation, were eager to obtain all the financial and professional help possible but they could not – or would not – see that this could only spring from spiritual work. Again, the Salvationists made it clear that there was no question of the Army coming into the area purely on social grounds, even if this would ensure registration. In an atmosphere of compromise, the Army had to stand firmly on principles.

These were anxious times. Days, weeks and months slipped past. Those observing from a distance were puzzled. If there was such great need and so many anxious to enlist the Army's help, why did the door not swing open? They could only see one side of the conflict which dogged the Gorbachev years. Some seemingly well-meaning groups wanted to hijack the Army's international credibility, yet themselves keep control. Others resented handing over scarce resources.

After many months of planning and negotiating for the use of an ideal property in central St Petersburg, just two votes cast by such people blocked an agreement between the Leningrad City Executive Council and the Army to transfer the building. Even after the official opening day there was still no security of tenure. The metaphorical revolving door which had baffled Karl Larsson 70 years previously was still relentlessly turning. New laws relating to religious groups required that a church needed 10 members in order to apply for registration. In the Army's case, a number of these, including Boris Bondarenko, would be adherents. Others who had helped sympathetically in all the Army's visits were invited to enlist. Added to these would be the overseas officers whose appointments to Russia were being finalised. A simple, yet significant, ceremony was held on Monday 6 May 1991 at the office of one of the Army's supporters. Verses from the Gospel of John were read before 15 people were enrolled as adherents of The Salvation Army. Asking God's blessing on each person, Lieut-Colonel Bjartveit handed them certificates of enrolment. The constitution, by now in its final form in both Russian and English, was read to this embryo Salvation Army and each adherent, two of whom in due course became soldiers, signed the Russian copy.

A few days later the precious papers were on the desk of General Eva Burrows in London. Standing round as she signed and sealed the document were some of the officers who had worked and prayed for this moment. They knew that this was but one step of many. Their prayers were still needed!

Finally Lieut-Colonel Bjartveit and Captain Peter Smith overcame the remaining problems and the constitution was registered at 5.30 pm on 28 May 1991 at the City Justice Department. At last the St Petersburg 'branch' of the 'Evangelical Christian Church of The Salvation Army' was official. The plans for the great day could go ahead with confidence.

Now that the situation was more secure the small band of officers and soldiers of the advance party were putting into action preparations which would acclimatise them for the new venture. The first to join the Bjartveits were Captain Sven-Erik Ljungholm and his wife, Kathy. The name Ljungholm had already appeared in the pages of Russian Salvation Army history. Gerda and Otto Ljungholm, who served for a few short months in Moscow in 1918, had a grandson, Sven-Erik. As a young boy he had been shown his grandmother's Army bonnet, with its red band bearing the unfamiliar words, *Armiya Spasseniya*, and other mementoes of her Russian adventure. He was fascinated. Russia to him was forbidden, hostile territory. To think that his grandparents had walked across Red Square and looked up at the Soviet stars on the top of the Kremlin spires! They had talked about Jesus to Russian people on street corners. Written in his Swedish mother tongue, Otto's diary for those months in Moscow was a precious family possession. It included a copy of the handbill advertising the very first Army meeting in Moscow on 17 October 1918, inviting people to come and hear Colonel Larsson. As Sven turned its pages, and read articles from *The Officer* magazine describing their work, he dreamed of going one day to continue what they had been forced to leave unfinished. At that time the fulfilment of his dream seemed the most unlikely thing in the world.

Years later Sven and Kathy noticed the small announcement in the Army's press asking for anyone who knew the Russian language and who would be open to service in the USSR to contact headquarters. So the dream was not so outlandish after all. By now auxiliary-captains of the USA Eastern Territory, the Ljungholms were stationed in Sweden. There was plenty for them to do in that field. They didn't feel the call was for them. But, just in case God had different ideas, they began to learn Russian. From then on there was a series of nudges which eventually led them to Moscow. After meeting Russians at the Swedish Foreign Ministry, Kathy, practical as ever, found herself making a list of people she knew would make a good team for working in Russia. It was an exciting thought. Then an American colleague, meeting Sven at the Army's 1990 congress in London, offered him Bibles for his work in Russia. 'But I'm working in Sweden, not Russia,' said the astonished Sven. Nevertheless, he took the Bibles, determined to think of a way to distribute them. That August he and Kathy travelled to St Petersburg for a weekend. Wearing Salvation Army uniform, they distributed the Bibles to people crowding along Nevsky Prospekt. Even a sharp summer thunderstorm did not deter them.

This experience had a deep effect on both of them as they felt the warmth of people who had been frozen out of the world for so many years. When Kathy took a group of junior soldiers from Malmö Corps to a congress in Copenhagen led by General Eva Burrows the two women talked about their common interest in Russia. It seemed logical to the General that Kathy and her husband should follow a family tradition and become part of the team when the Army moved into Russia again. Kathy was non-committal. 'It's up to God and you!' she replied to this suggestion. Sven, too, was not over-enthusiastic. Introduced to Commissioner Gauntlett in the lunch queue at International Headquarters during a visit to London to purchase uniforms, he talked about his experiences and they compared notes.

Quite soon, an official offer was made: if you want to go to Russia, it will be arranged. The Ljungholms were in a quandary. They felt settled in their Swedish corps appointment but if marching orders were given they would comply. So it was that Sven joined John Bjartveit in 1991 for the February visit to

Leningrad. Later it was proposed that the Ljungholms would have responsibility for developing social work there before moving on to open work in Moscow when this was feasible. They arranged to stay a month in Moscow from 15 May to join an intensive Russian language course. This time would also give them the opportunity to make arrangements for the Oslo Temple Band's witness in Moscow and to search in museums and libraries for any references to The Salvation Army. At the end of the month they returned home for furlough with some idea of what might face them in the future. It was a daunting, yet exciting prospect.

Away in Canada, the third officer-couple, Lieutenants Geoff and Sandra Ryan, were packing cases and boxes to despatch to St Petersburg. Sandra's visit in 1990 with the Canadian delegation had given her some idea of what to expect. She and her husband had been appointed to Newfoundland from college. Far away from sophisticated cities and Salvation Army headquarters, they had learnt what it meant to be self-sufficient and to make things work without the close back-up of a team of colleagues. Adjusting to the maritime climate with its severe winter was also good preparation. Tucked in among clothing and household goods were many books, music copies and visual aids. A guitar, timbrel and keyboard were essential. A computer went in too. Building a corps for people with little, if any, knowledge of the Bible would need thorough preaching and teaching as well as a loving pastoral ministry. Music would be a common language and an inspiration for worship. The young couple had also grappled with the Cyrillic alphabet and were beginning to get their tongues around the unfamiliar language.

The long days of June passed anxiously for John Bjartveit. Would the plans fall into place? Visas had been applied for in good faith. A large building had been booked. Leaflets and posters advertising the Army's advent were ready for distribution. Many Russians, including the Army's solicitor, had left the city for the summer break – and still there was no certainty of being able to retain buildings for use as offices, homes or meeting halls. The other members of the team were not due to arrive until the week of the opening date. It was quite a test of faith!

But the day on which the tall figure of Sven Ljungholm stepped out across the forecourt of the Winter Palace holding aloft Norway's gift of a bright new Salvation Army flag with the Russian motto, to the strains of Oslo Temple Band, was a day of faith triumphant! The General, commissioners, colonels, captains, lieutenants and soldiers, minds awhirl with the wonder of it all, marched in step across stones which had witnessed countless parades. Some sensed strong echoes of the past as they glanced at the second flag, the old one which had flown in the city years before. Cameras clicked and whirred and questions buzzed. '*Sto-eta?*' – 'What is it?' Many in the crowd knew. They had seen Salvationists on television, read about them in the newspaper or studied the leaflets. They passed on their knowledge: 'It's The Salvation Army, a Christian Army of peace.'

At this time of discovery, Russians were rather like small children in Santa's cave. Their drab, predictable life had suddenly been transformed as the world crowded in to help – or to exploit. How could they know which offers were genuine? Only by trying every offer. Thus crowds attended meetings and festivals held in St Petersburg that weekend, 6 and 7 July, attracted by joyful music and happy faces. A Baptist choir and a smaller Christian music group added a distinctly Russian flavour. The gospel message, too, was eagerly absorbed and the reverent response, reflecting the Orthodox sense of repentance and awe, especially moved those who witnessed Russian spirituality for the first time. At the public reopening meeting held at Yubileiny Sports Palace, the deputy mayor of the city, Igor Kucherenko, expressed the thoughts of many when he said, 'For 70 years Christianity has been persecuted in this country, but we have kept the faith in our hearts.'

Glorious weather enhanced the open-air meetings, one of which took place outside the building the Army still hoped to use. Encouraged by the presence of friends and officials whose help had enabled this historic moment to happen, and exhilarated by the sense of the Holy Spirit's blessing, the General left the small group with the assurance of her prayers. Speaking to *Salvationist* on her return to London she mentioned the six officers who had the great responsibility of beginning to build a Russian Salvation Army. 'They will need our prayers,' she said, adding that the problems were vast, but every contribution of love and care would be something of value for the people of the Russia and the CIS. Oslo Temple Band moved on to Moscow with Captain and Mrs Ljungholm. Here their ministry was in two large hospitals to patients who crowded to the windows of their drab wards and smiled broadly as music rose to meet them. Adherents who had been recruited during the Ljungholms' previous visits were kept busy distributing copies of the Gospels both in the hospitals and also among the crowds who paused to listen to the band when it played in central Moscow squares and parks. Further opportunities for Christian witness came during a service held in a Baptist church and a festival in the Olympic village. In all, thousands of Muscovites were made aware of the Army's message in a few short hours.

Chapter 6

LAYING FOUNDATIONS

The adventure of starting again

AFTER the glory of these days the following weeks felt a little unreal. Now carefully thought-out plans had to be actioned in conditions which were at best unfamiliar and at worst hostile. Daily life was a struggle. Shopping for basic food supplies took far longer than the expatriates had been used to. Cars and minibuses manufactured for smooth roads soon showed signs of wear from the potholed streets. In addition to adjusting to these conditions, team members had to discover and accept each other's strengths and weaknesses and learn to work together. Perhaps the greatest stress was the fact that the whole Army world had large expectations. The seven Salvationists were in the spotlight, and could easily be dazzled if they took their eyes from the task.

The group soon discovered that it was no use waiting for ideal conditions before starting any programme. Their job description had emphasised adaptability, empathy and energy. Soon Leningrad Corps was taking shape. The foundations were built on prayer. Names and, where known, circumstances of more than 150 of those contacted during the opening celebrations had been collated into a valuable document which became a focus for the team's morning prayer. Where special needs were identified, people were visited in their homes. This sensitive ministry to people whose doors were seldom opened to strangers, let alone foreigners, was a vital factor in establishing the corps.

Those visited were among the many who, attracted by this new expression of Christianity, accepted personal invitations to attend the first corps meeting held on 21 July 1991. The hall, loaned by the local Baptist church, was packed. The Army flag given by General Burrows, a copper Army crest from South African Salvationists and flowers placed in memory of those who served in Russia in the early years of the century, set the scene. A moving testimony given by Maria Tschushinova, a Baptist who had met Jesus at an Army Sunday school as a child, and music – computerised – gave more Army flavour. As people left the hall their expressions reflected a variety of reactions. Some were quizzically amused; others were enigmatic or set in stern, introverted lines; but many reflected the brightness of the smiles of those who had come to show God's love in action.

After a week or two the large Lenin-Sovieta Palace of Culture on Kirovski Prospekt was hired, with plenty of room for everyone. Here in an upper room a pattern for worship and fellowship was quickly established. Russian Christians as well as team members were involved in ministry, and people who knew nothing about the Christian faith listened eagerly. New people arrived weekly. For some, one visit was enough to satisfy their curiosity and they never came again, but others were sensitive to God's Spirit. At first it was felt that a mercy seat was not appropriate because adequate counselling would be impossible. Instead, after a time of quiet reflection at the end of the address, the invitation was given for those who wished to know more about the faith to remain behind for a personal conversation when the rest of the congregation moved out of the hall. In this way many took the first step of faith.

As people chatted after the meeting, enjoying buns and tea, the nurture of each new seeker began with friendly words and an invitation to attend Bible classes. Within a few weeks a busy programme was scheduled – open-air meetings, seminars to explain the Army's doctrines, Bible studies, hospital visits, music practice. Musicians, military bandsmen among them, recognised a new way in which their skills could be used. People were eager to belong, to be involved. They sensed this was a good thing. It was a way of learning and serving, building the new society they longed for. Some would have donned the uniform there and then.

Knowing the importance of thorough grounding in the Christian life, the Ryans set to work preparing teaching material for both adults and children. Working hand to mouth, this was selected, translated by Minna Karlström and other staff members, photocopied and used. The supplies trailer which came regularly from Norway always brought more paper in addition to food, clothing and medical supplies. It was hoped that by September a number of adherents would be publicly recognised.

Soon it became time to hold soldiership preparation classes for those who seemed ready for this further commitment. More lessons to produce! John Coutts came on 'holiday' to the city with his wife, Heather, and son and translated Major Chick Yuill's *Battle Orders*. From that time on there would be a continuous process – as one group of adherents were enrolled, some then becoming recruits and moving on to the next stage of preparing for soldiership, another group would begin the course. Those with the aptitude – some just teenagers – were being trained to teach children, using helpful leaflets which took the gospel message into children's homes and hospitals.

The visit of a group of students from Norway's Jeløy Folk High School proved to be valuable both for the students, who broadened their horizons, and for the Russians, who enjoyed making more links with The Salvation Army international family as they worked and worshipped together for a few days. One young Russian, Vikka, became a student at Jeløy the following year.

Still not fully adjusted to such extreme changes in lifestyle, and immersed in the demanding activities of a growing church, team members had little time to notice what was happening on the political scene. The events of a few days in the third week of August took the world by surprise too.

John and Heather Coutts were still in the city, supporting the officers with interpreting, teaching, escorting children on excursions, and enjoying it all. One morning John tuned into the BBC World Service. It was 9 o'clock on 19 August. He heard crackling the scary announcement which was sending shock waves round the world: 'President Gorbachev has been deposed.' It was almost unthinkable. Was all that had been achieved in vain?

Knowing and partly knowing, the team stopped everything and prayed. 'Lord, no matter what unforeseen circumstances the day may bring, help me to meet them with a tranquil mind.' The words, so apt, were those of a prayer penned by an elder of the Optina Monastery. They had been given to John Coutts by one of the adherents after the Sunday meeting.

It was difficult to be tranquil in the days that followed. If the expatriates were downcast, the Russians were more so, with good reason. They hardly dared voice their fears. Would the nation slither back down the slope of progress and freedom they had been struggling with such effort to mount?

Gradually, news that the attempted coup had failed due to the intervention of Boris Yeltsin filtered through, and summer life went on, although the balance of political power had changed. John and his family travelled to Moscow as planned, witnessing the strange combination of abandoned barricades and curious tourists on the banks of the Moscow River. Meanwhile, Leningrad Corps, after a moment's hiatus, marched on. Whether Yeltsin would be a friend or foe to The Salvation Army was yet to be discovered.

Autumn brought more stability to the corps as people returned from country dachas, and school term began. Opportunities for open-air ministry were grasped firmly before winter set in. These were made more effective by the music of a small brass band formed, by special permission, from officers supplemented by professional musicians and military bandsmen, using instruments donated by Valby Corps, in Denmark. The band was welcomed enthusiastically by the congregation on the last Sunday in September. With added verve, they sang a new song to the Lord.

Not everyone who came into the meetings shared this positive enthusiasm. There were critics, sceptics and those with even stronger antagonistic views. It was obvious that Satan was badly shaken by this resurgence of Christian faith. Sometimes practical things threatened to dismay – unheated rooms, locked doors, missing equipment – but Russians are tough! Cold? Put on more clothes! Locked out? Use the corridor! Missing equipment? Improvise! *Niet* problem!

The Ljungholms, as well as actively supporting the corps, had their own agenda in the social field, strengthening links already forged in previous visits to the city. It was impossible to meet every need, although quantities of humanitarian aid were being channelled through The Salvation Army. They felt that one thing they could do was attempt to co-ordinate the efforts of more than a hundred philanthropic organisations which had sprung up in the city. A conference was held in October but it became obvious that this was a long-term process and they would not have time to consolidate the scheme before moving to Moscow. Another concern was that university departments were beginning to develop social work courses with very little experience on which to base the curriculum. Sven prepared a handbook of guidance, based on Western principles, and had a number of opportunities to introduce these ideas to tutors and students.

There was work to be done at pavement level too. Scores of children with no home but abandoned buildings roamed the streets in all weathers. Mother Theresa's Sisters of Charity were doing what they could to help, and the Army provided a soup run. Many of these children were on the streets because their parents were in prison. A vital ministry was needed there, too.

The suggestion of introducing a prison-release programme to help men and women re-establish themselves in society was planted in the minds of responsible officials and a long-term plan to provide accommodation for ex-prisoners was proposed. The very idea that prisoners deserved care was not easy for Russians to assimilate. They were locked away with the bare minimum of human comfort. Official brutality was no longer the norm, but neglect and lack of resources had taken their toll on many lives.

Even hospitals were severely ill-equipped. Gifts sent from other countries were more than welcome, but in no way met the need. Typhoid and cholera, scourges of the past, had been replaced by a new horror – Aids. The Ljungholms were especially concerned with the children affected by this condition. During one hospital visit they came across distraught parents alone in the car park, clutching the clothes of their child who had just died. They had waited for an hour and a half for the undertaker to come, with no help or comfort. Because Aids was even more of a taboo in Russia than in the West, it was as if their child had never existed.

Out of the cases of Aids documented in Russia, the vast majority were recorded in Volgograd. Twice the Ljungholms visited this city in the course of a year. At the hospital, where half the Aids patients treated were children, they saw that syringes were badly needed to prevent further contamination from old needles. Arrangements were made to bring a consignment from Sweden by road. An international company supplied drugs in liquid form – a great improvement. Sven and Kathy introduced a support programme, explaining away myths about the disease and helping parents come to terms with the facts. Their practical ministry was respected by medical staff as well as patients. There was fertile ground in Volgograd when the Army came later to plant a corps.

Moved by these experiences, Sven and Kathy developed a service in Leningrad too, counselling bewildered parents and arranging special treats to bring some joy into the short lives of their children. Even the most disabled were included. Coaches were hired and naval cadets recruited to lift heavy wheelchairs so that children could visit the circus or take a sightseeing trip. It was worth it just to see wan faces glowing with excitement.

So many aspects of Leningrad life in 1991 were reflections of conditions in the 1920s. Food was rationed, with blue-collar workers given priority over professionals. That was not often a great benefit – there was very little food in the shops, however many rations were allocated. Petrol queues, bread queues, potato queues, queues for bus and tram were all part of everyday life. The officers at first had small self-contained apartments in the Chaika Hotel, catering for themselves. The Bjartveits used the corridor as an office, had a photocopier in their bedroom and the fax machine in the sitting room! All the staff crowded into their kitchen for lunch each workday. The other apartments also doubled as offices and there was little space – or time, come to that – to relax.

Although rents seemed very reasonable at first, compared with those in the West, rapid inflation soon changed this. A high rent was paid for Sunday activities, but the Children's Fund generously made space, rent free, during the week. After hours, their office and adjacent corridor were used for the corps programme. One evening it was band practice, another, Christian teaching. On Tuesdays the corps ran a feeding programme, delivering soup and bread to the homes of disabled people in conjunction with an 'invalids association' who supplied the contacts. Encouraged by the arrangement, the association took full responsibility for this scheme after a while. In addition, needy people came regularly to the storehouse for food. It was a nomadic existence but, in spite of all the inconvenience, the corps grew and people came to know the Lord.

When the severe winter weather prevented effective open-air ministry, the corps used the time to visit hospital patients. One of the recruits made arrangements to visit a number of hospitals in turn on Friday evenings, alternating with 'Sunday school' at a children's hospital. Music, testimony and a printed gospel message brought a healing touch to those who had little else to look forward to. As Christmas approached volunteers prepared 2,000 small gift bags – appropriately known as 'sunshine bags' – to take to a number of children's hospitals in the city. When December came they would distribute the gifts and, skilfully woven into some entertainment, tell the story of the first Christmas using pictures and puppets. There were so many avenues of service opening and the officers and their people let no opportunity pass.

Far to the south, on the Black Sea coast, unbeknown to the rest of the Army world, a soldier sworn in as a member of the Petrograd VII corps in 1918 was leading his own outpost. Hearing that the Army was re-established in Leningrad, 'General' Vladimir Mikhailovich – as he was locally known – made a phone call. Captain Ljungholm who took the call was, to say the least, surprised to discover that the general on the line was not General Eva Burrows! Could the man's story be genuine? Sven decided that he and Kathy should go to Yalta and see for themselves.

The tall figure of Vladimir stood out in the crowd on the airport tarmac. His firm clasp as he and Sven shook hands confirmed his strong character. 'It was an emotional and gripping moment for me to meet and shake the hand of a man who had served in St Petersburg at the side of Adjutant and Mrs Otto Ljungholm, my grandparents,' wrote Sven in *Salvationist*. The 'General' had made part of his rambling home into a headquarters. Seated there, high above the coast where privileged Russians had for years enjoyed lavish holidays, Vladimir told his story.

As a boy he had been attracted by the Army and was soon involved in helping to distribute food in the stricken community. When the Army encountered severe difficulties he, like many others, wanted to keep the spirit of the Movement alive. Travelling to the Crimea he managed for a while to send food supplies from this more-productive area to his colleagues in the city. The charitable work Vladimir and his band of followers did for many years, especially during the Second World War, eventually earned him a sentence in Siberia for 'actions against the State'. This dark period in his life he found difficult to talk about but other exiled people have spoken for him.

Taking his cue from an *Izvestia* article reporting that The Salvation Army was hoping to be re-established in the USSR, the 'General' decided to make his branch official. The Ljungholms met several of the 20 soldiers who had identified with their elderly, yet still determined, leader. Meeting this even taller officer and his wife, naturally Vladimir made his requests! The soldiers would like uniforms. Blankets (yes, it can be cold in Yalta), food, toys and Bibles would be very welcome. The Ljungholms, knowing their own limitations, as well as the need to respect procedures, promised to do their best. In fact an 'official' corps was in due time established in Yalta, and Vladimir Mikhailovich was awarded the Order of the Founder in acknowledgement of his faithfulness through the years. The news of this small group waving the Army flag so far away was encouraging. It was proof that God keeps faith with those who honour him. Seldom do those who sow see the whole harvest of their efforts, but sometimes it exceeds all they might hope for.

The Ljungholms were preparing for the move to Moscow by handing over their social programme to the officers who would remain in Leningrad – or St Petersburg as the city was now to be called again. Russian recruits soon understood the Army philosophy that Christians are saved to serve and quickly became involved in every aspect of ministry.

Chapter 7

ECHOES OF THE PAST

Meeting need in Russia's cities

WORKING in cramped conditions, Mrs Lieut-Colonel Bjørg Bjartveit and her helpers did what they could to care for needy people. Their little store was a place of miracles. Just as it seemed the supply was running out, a new gift would be received and more people could be invited to come for assistance. The local authority had provided a ground floor room in Bolshoi Prospekt for storage, close to other offices, so it was impractical to have the usual queue waiting to be served. To improve the situation, an appointment system was introduced. People telephoned the office – local calls were free – and were given a time to attend. A card index was compiled to ensure fair distribution and continuing contact.

In this way 40 or 50 families, some with seven or eight children to feed and clothe on an income which inflation had made totally inadequate, were given practical help each day. Food, clothes, shoes and sometimes toys were carried away in bulging plastic bags by grateful people. Ex-prisoners and others, who were destitute if they had no family to turn to, were also glad of help. Some felt a pang of hurt pride, but nevertheless they were grateful. Perhaps the situation would improve, but for now they had to accept things as they were.

Warehousing for lorry-loads of supplies still arriving from a variety of sources was provided at the First Medical Institute in return for help given to the hospital over many months. Heavy boxes of tinned meat, porridge oats, coffee, second-hand clothing, shoes, hospital equipment and medicines were unloaded by willing volunteers and carefully stored and distributed. Once again the Army in Leningrad was a crucial link between a great need and those whose concern moved them to meet it, playing a small but effective part in an international humanitarian operation.

The move into Moscow was personally significant to Sven Ljungholm, linking him as it did with his family's past. Since working in Russia he and his wife had regularly visited the city, forging links they hoped would be productive. They even had an apartment which had been vacated in a hurry by a Muscovite who eventually settled abroad, and had offered his home to the Army for the use of officers. When the Ljungholms moved in on 1 November 1991 they were faced with evidence of the hurriedness of the exit of the previous occupants, but this was a minor problem compared with others they would face in giving the Army a foothold in the historic city.

An experienced businessman, Sven went about the task in true entrepreneurial style. He thought big. There was still keen interest in anything new. Moscow, the seat of government where Communism had been entrenched, was, if anything, slower to open doors to new ideas than St Petersburg, which was geographically and culturally closer to the West. But the trickle of perestroika had become a flood and there was every evidence that people in Moscow would respond to evangelism. Within a month Sven held a press conference, explaining plans for motivating and enabling Russian people to help each other. Working from an office in the Youth Institute he built on good relationships he had made with the rector and then targeted the young generation who were studying in the sociology faculty. They were learning new theories.

He would give them opportunity to see theory in practice and, he hoped, become involved themselves.

People queuing in the snow for meagre supplies were a common sight here, as well as in St Petersburg. Regional authorities had good facilities for providing elderly citizens and others unable to fend for themselves with nourishing hot meals. But these *stolovars* were dark and empty and the staff were paid to stay at home. There was no food to cook. Here was a practical way in which the Army could make a contribution.

Large quantities of humanitarian aid from Sweden and Britain, together with 18,000 tonnes from the USA, much of it through SAWSO (Salvation Army World Service Office), were allocated to the Army to distribute mainly to elderly people. While politicians were disputing different methods of reforming industry and agriculture, moving away from complete State control, these huge structures themselves almost disintegrated. Thousands were thrown out of work. Those with jobs sometimes went for weeks without pay. Savings lost value as inflation zoomed upwards, increasing 720 per cent. Those on pensions almost despaired. Even basic foodstuffs became scarce and expensive.

If the Army was to play a part in relieving hunger in Moscow more than two people were needed, and there were many who had already caught the spirit of these Americans who swept them into action. Ludmilla, a fine teacher whose salary was so low that she could not manage, was given the responsible task of supervising the main warehouse. She was effective in this job, too. It was not easy to control the movement of stores which would be very profitable on the black market. She conscientiously served the Army in this capacity for a long while.

Then there was tall student Katya, and her mother, a senior lecturer at the Youth Institute, who had worked to educate young people in the Communist ideology but now saw what had been missing. The motivation and methods of The Salvation Army caught their interest. It was sociology with compassion. The social workers of the future would benefit from learning about it. Katya, a fluent English speaker, was invaluable as an interpreter and translator. Although still in her teens, she assisted at influential conferences and consultations in a mature manner, enabling Army leaders to maximise the contacts they made.

Quickly the group worked towards an agreement with the local authority. The Army would provide food for a *stolovar*. Its staff would be recalled, the facilities prepared, and more than 200 elderly people would come for a nourishing meal at least once a week. By Christmas the plan had been put into action. It was an important step in co-operation and understanding. Before long, the pattern was repeated in 14 more *stolovars*. Informed by newspaper advertisements, through support groups or the office of the local prefect (administrator), customers came in crowds. By then there were volunteers from the new corps who gave time to befriend those people who needed companionship and care as much as borsch and bread.

Although social service was much needed, it was even more necessary to establish a worshipping community which would nurture Christians and motivate them to serve their neighbours. It would not always be possible – or desirable – to rely on help from outside the country. Booking a hall which had been used by his grandparents, and distributing similar leaflets of invitation, Captain Ljungholm and his wife waited for people to arrive. It was quite a large hall. Would the congregation be embarrassingly sparse? They felt less uneasy when a portrait of the unsmiling Lenin was covered with the Army tricolour flag!

They need not have worried. When the meeting was due to begin it was standing-room only. Those who had already associated themselves with the Army welcomed many new people. Then, to the distant sounds of a grand piano in the next room, the people sang. The Army had come alive again in Moscow.

Wasting no time, recruits classes were begun. By the end of December more than 50 people were interested in becoming soldiers. Scientists and schoolboys, bakers and babushkas, typists and truck drivers, artists and artisans – representatives of a cross-section of Moscow society – had investigated and then integrated into this new expression of faith which had been allowed through an open door. The corps had no place to call its own, but people bonded in spite of this, travelling on metro or bus from one venue to another for meetings, classes and practices. More than one soldier of the corps had become involved with the Army as a result of a chance meeting with a Salvationist at a bus stop.

New Year celebrations in 1992 had an added dimension. Salvationists told young people the simple story of Bethlehem, many of them hearing it for the first time. The Christ child was being acknowledged in a city where church bells had been silenced for some 70 years.

Back in St Petersburg, New Year was celebrated with the first enrolment of soldiers of the resurrected corps. Nineteen smartly-uniformed soldiers received illuminated copies of the articles of war to commemorate this occasion which was of such significance for The Salvation Army as a whole as well as for each individual. Their friends expressed congratulations traditionally by presenting each new soldier with a single carnation.

The soldiers represented a cross section of society. Julie, aged 21, had been searching for the right place in which her new understanding of the Christian faith could grow. In spite of initial misunderstanding at home she felt that by becoming a soldier she was in the centre of God's will. 'I've joined a family of Christian people and I really love them,' she said. Julie dedicated her life and capabilities to God as she stood beneath the Army flag.

Standing by her was 53-year-old journalist and poet, Vadim. Life had not been easy for him as he grappled with conflicting philosophies in an alien culture. Now he prayed for a deeper understanding of God's will and plan for his life, a plan which had opened up to new freedoms, allowing him the privilege of being a soldier of the Lord Jesus Christ.

Then there was Nina. Perhaps her story was the most remarkable of all. She was born in Belorussia but when she was 20 years old her family went to live in Finland. In the early 1940s she met The Salvation Army and soon became involved at a corps. Enthusiasm there was contagious, and she became a soldier, eventually going to college in Helsinki to train as a Salvation Army officer. Sadly, her training was interrupted by war and all those of Russian birth had to leave Finland. The Army had been proscribed in Russia long before and Nina was left without the support of Christian fellowship. Throughout the years, as she married and brought up two children, she remained faithful in her soul, patiently working out her calling in a very restricted way. When she discovered that people in the familiar uniform were in the streets of Petrograd again, Nina made sure she attended the first public meeting. It felt wonderful! She could hardly wait to tell the young officers that she too was a Salvationist. Rather sceptically Lieutenant Ryan wrote down her name. Many years had passed – could he corroborate her claim?

Enquiries were made in Finland. Yes, there were soldiers rolls from the time in question, and there was her name – Nina Korotkaja! So it was that the 1992 soldiers roll of the Petrograd corps was opened with the names of 19 newly-enrolled soldiers, most of them new to faith, and one transfer who would soon celebrate 50 years as a Christian. Those with vision could see how important this moment was for each soldier and for the Army in Russia. Future Sunday-school teachers, translators, officers and social workers were all among that group.

One of the soldiers was the manager of the tramway and had used his position to initiate an effective form of witness. 'Have you seen the Salvation Army tram?' people were soon asking each other. Sure enough, trundling along the tracks was a newly-painted tram, drawing attention by its very brightness. On the sides were slogans, an unusual feature in pre-glasnost days. 'With heart to God and hand to man' declared one message. The other invited, 'Come to me, all who labour and are heavy laden, and I will give you rest.' In smaller letters, details of corps meetings were given. The 'hallelujah tram' spread the word in St Petersburg for a year. There was no doubt that The Salvation Army was in town!

With all the publicity more and more people knew where to go for practical help as well as Christian worship and teaching, so staff at the small delivery centre were always busy. Since Mrs Bjartveit had taken over the task when the Ljungholms left for Moscow she had been fully occupied there and other tasks were neglected, so she was delighted when Major and Mrs George Whittingham from the United Kingdom Territory gave a month of their time to relieve her for a while. Their previous experience in emergency relief work was good preparation for the job. When they returned home they became ambassadors for their new friends, advising willing donors of the best ways in which they could help Salvationists in former Eastern bloc countries.

The Army was making an impact in the medical sphere too. In February, Captain Ljungholm's concern that Russians should be helped to deal with the Aids menace resulted in a three-day conference co-ordinated by IHQ's Chief Medical Adviser, Captain (Dr) Ian Campbell. Doctors came to the government Aids clinic from all over Russia to discuss clinical care, counselling, education and administration, learning new skills to combat this 20th-century plague. Spiritual aspects of the care of patients and their families were not forgotten. The specialists had much to think about as they returned to their hospitals and passed on new experiences. For some, the responsibility to see beyond the medical condition to the holistic treatment of a patient was a new and challenging idea. Two other Aids conferences were also held that year.

The traditional rivalry between St Petersburg and Moscow to some extent affected The Salvation Army, largely to its benefit. The younger sibling corps had an example to follow. It could learn from the successes and failures which had been experienced in St Petersburg.

One important aspect to which this applied was negotiating the Army's legal standing. After much effort the constitution had been signed in St Petersburg and then was successfully adapted for Moscow. On 8 March, Lieut-Colonel Bjartveit called the required constitution meeting and, guided by Captain Peter Smith from International Headquarters and the Army's Russian solicitor, representative members of the congregation signed the document which would be ratified two months later.

Ever since corps were reopened in St Petersburg and Moscow, Salvationists have travelled on the overnight train between the two cities, sharing special events in friendship and encouragement. Still feeling the glow of their own enrolment day just two months previously, soldiers from St Petersburg made that journey in March to welcome their brothers and sisters in Moscow as they too made their vows under the Army flag. General Eva Burrows had travelled there, and leaders from Norway and St Petersburg joined her. To witness new Christians committing themselves to service in The Salvation Army is a moving experience in any place. As the stage filled with men and women kneeling to sign the articles of war in a hall where, until recently, a godless creed had been propagated, emotion was tangible.

'Russian people are a thinking people who want to know the deep things of life,' the General had said. The response of many in the congregation to the gospel challenge proved her right. Soldiers from St Petersburg, faith growing moment by moment, moved forward to counsel these seekers. Now no language barrier hindered the work of the Holy Spirit! Bandsmen from Boscombe, UK, bringing humanitarian aid by truck, harmonised with Baptists from Moscow and the congregation from too many places to count, praising God for allowing them to witness this moment.

Public interest was stirred and the General used every possible opportunity to make the Army and its purpose widely known, including a press conference where she shared the rostrum with the deputy minister involved in the government's social programme.

A somewhat sceptical journalist asked why Russians would want to join the Army. Sensing his mood, General Burrows turned to her translator, one of the newly-enrolled soldiers. 'Well, Olga?' she prompted. 'There was a stunned and respectful silence among the journalists and cameramen as the 18-year-old university student, Olga Barykina, testified that Christ had given her so much that she wanted to serve him and do something for him and for others,' wrote the International Under-Secretary for Europe, Lieut-Colonel Miriam Frederiksen, reporting for *Salvationist*. The events she was recording were especially significant for Miriam, the granddaughter of Karl Larsson whose Russian experience had been told to her when a child.

Anxious that understanding and co-operation should be maintained among the many expressions of Christianity now invading Russia, the General appreciated the reception given to her by Patriarch Alexi, head of the Orthodox Church in Moscow. This meeting in the beautiful Novodevichy Convent on the banks of the Moscow River was a short, formal occasion, but the fact that it took place at all was encouraging. Progressive Orthodox priests were keen to enlarge and modernise their ministry and this was a sign of recognition of new ideas.

Before the weekend was out, Captain Ljungholm's office staff had produced the first corps newsletter, the forerunner of a revived *Vestnik Spasseniya* which he hoped would be on the streets before long. New freedom of the press had led to a flutter of new papers in the cities. The 'white-winged messenger' must be among them! Sven, on the lookout for an editor, scrutinised likely people who arrived at the hall. He didn't have to wait long. A Moscow news editor sent a rather reluctant journalist to report on this new group which was causing such a stir. Svetlana had been most irritated to be woken early one Sunday morning by a phone call summoning her to work. A religious meeting, the boss had said. Now if it had been a theatre preview or a literary conference she would have been keen, but this military thing wasn't her scene. Still, she had to go, if she wanted to keep her job. There was not much work-security in the time of glasnost.

Notebook in hand, Svetlana sat in the hall becoming more and more enthralled. There were people of all ages, not just babushkas, who were usually the only ones associated with religion. Smartly-uniformed people played their parts purposefully. The singing was professional and the preaching powerful and thought-provoking. Patiently waiting her moment after the meeting, she managed a word or two with the tall, American leader who had impressed her so much. The social work he briefly spoke of interested Svetlana too.

Next day she filed an enthusiastic report to the editor. Her duty was done – but her service was just beginning. Almost instantly she was given the job of editing the Moscow Corps newsletter *Moscow Salvation Front,* which appeared dated March 1992. Before many weeks had passed, Svetlana was a uniformed Salvationist, with responsibility for the revived *Vestnik Spasseniya,* a post she held for a number of years.

Sven's other plan for Salvation Army input into social services education had been formulated as a month's teaching programme in various institutes staffed by a small team of officers from England. It was launched by a conference at which General Burrows, before returning to London, gave a keynote address, pointing out again the Army's interlinked roles of church and charity. It was up to Mrs Commissioner Rosemarie Fullarton, Mrs Major Diane Boyd and Captain Joseph Smith to interpret this concept and turn it into a reality which young people would understand and accept. They found this quite a task!

Hard as it is to believe when meeting warm-hearted Russian friends, there had for years been a USSR policy to prevent people being kind. The word 'charity' almost disappeared from the language. The cold war affected internal as well as external relationships. Arriving in Russia with ordered minds and long experience of social policies in the West, the three officers soon found they were thinking on their feet as they faced group after group of young people with a totally different heritage. The collective diary they kept tells of minor tragedies which befell these three innocents abroad and major triumphs of response and communication with impressionable students and influential professors from many parts of the country.

Education in the Soviet Union was very formal in style, and even such a basic thing as writing paper was scarce.The interactive methods introduced by the team members came as a shock but they persevered and gradually they felt that ideas were filtering through.

The month passed in a whirl of seminars, lectures, forums and interviews, with sightseeing for good measure. At the end they could understand the breadth of Sven's Ljungholm's vision but they also knew that it would be a long-term project needing carefully defined priorities. Moscow, let alone St Petersburg, Volgograd, Yalta and the rest of the CIS, could not be rebuilt in a day. They thanked God for allowing them to share the vision and to play some part in laying a foundation.

After this demanding period of expansion it was time for some of the pioneers to take a break. Sven and Kathy Ljungholm handed over to Commissioner Ingrid Lindberg, now retired, who was thrilled to see the development of the work since she had visited the small exhibition in the Charity Society's headquarters. Helped by Canadian Danielle Strickland, a Salvationist of Brampton Corps who was already well-immersed in teaching the children, Commissioner shepherded the flock, discovering their personalities and needs and earning their love and respect. The fact that Major and Mrs George Whittingham came for two weeks to supervise the busy social programme freed her to do this pastoral work. The corps was growing so big that there was a danger of soldiers being strangers to each other. They were people from a great variety of backgrounds. Many were well-educated people who were attracted by new ideas, by the English language, which they often spoke fluently, and opportunities to travel. Others had experienced few privileges under the old system. Ingrid was determined that they should not feel inferior within the Christian family. She presented Bible study and recruits classes carefully so that everyone's needs were satisfied. As soon as they were ready, each person was given opportunities for service – hospital visitation, prison ministry, serving soup to homeless people at mainline stations, teaching children in Sunday school, serving in the *stolovars*, preparing music for worship, unloading trucks, preparing leaflets – there was no end to the work to be done.

The lively, exciting springtime of the corps gradually moved on towards the maturity and fruitfulness of summer. More experienced officers from overseas were needed to maximise this time of tremendous growth but, meantime, potential leaders could be identified among the Russian soldiers who were to prove themselves again and again.

The numerical growth of both St Petersburg and Moscow Corps was quite phenomenal. As soon as one group of recruits became uniformed soldiers another crowd took their place at recruits classes, attending regularly and delving eagerly into their new-found treasure, the Bible. Paperback Testaments which had been freely distributed were already outworn, but new Christian publishers were issuing study books and hardback Bibles which were purchased when resources allowed. Children were also taught and trained, provided with uniform and given opportunities for service.

One reason for this progress was natural enthusiasm for something new, especially something which had been consistently repressed for two generations. The way in which Salvationists, recognising the demoralised state of the country, set to work to improve things, also appealed. Many Russians longed to do something. Here were leaders and resources, and they were ready to help. The international status of the movement gave them confidence and they were happy to wear a uniform which identified them with a widely-respected Christian church. They recognised that the new flag they followed symbolised the same God revered by the Orthodox Church and represented by ancient icons in dark corners of many homes.

Commissioner Lindberg led the corps into the open air during the warm days of early summer. Some coming straight from work or college changed into uniform in the shelter of bushes in Gorki Park! Testimony, children's singing and old Russian hymns drew the attention of people enjoying a respite from concrete estates and dusty yards. Crowds stopped to listen to the word of God. Like those who listened to the same words on a Galilean hillside almost 2,000 years before, sometimes the word fell on the rocky ground of unbelief, or was choked by thistles of self-interest. Others accepted the truth eagerly, without deep understanding and it was soon forgotten when other new interests demanded attention. But there were those who in years to come enjoyed a harvest of blessing, both given and received. The faithful witness of those Salvationists under the trees would not be in vain.

The Ryans also had handed over responsibility of the St Petersburg Corps for a short time to John Norton, a member of a team of young Canadian Salvationists led by Major and Mrs David Hiscock, who had worked in the two cities gaining valuable experience in evangelism. Geoff and Sandra spent 10 days in England, scarcely resting but enthusing many Army friends with the wonderful way God was working in their corps. They returned in good time for the second enrolment of senior and junior soldiers.

Of the 200 people on average attending both senior meetings and Sunday school in St Petersburg, a good percentage came regularly and sincerely, growing in faith and understanding. A new venue had been found for children's work. Now teaching could be given in five different age groups after a lively session all together. Young Russians, many of them students, gave time to prepare themselves to teach these groups, crowding into the officers' quarters to develop the arts of puppetry, poster-writing and drama.

Their own spiritual growth was stimulated as they led children to discover Jesus as their friend and saviour.

The summer break in the UK academic year enabled John and Heather Coutts to return to St Petersburg, relieving the Ryans for a holiday. They occupied themselves collecting broth from a restaurant for a soup run, leading a three-week Bible study attended by 70 eager students, purchasing a supply of serviceable children's shoes from a factory and still finding time for a tourist visit to Pushkin. They witnessed the process of choosing a corps council, necessary in Russian law, when the Ryans returned. It had been an inspiring, if not relaxing, holiday.

Major and Mrs Chick Yuill from the UK led a three-day residential retreat for 80 young people, a valuable opportunity to question, evaluate and confirm what had been so rapidly absorbed during the year.

One year. So much had happened. Those who attended the two Russian corps had the benefits of as full a programme as most Army centres which had existed for 100 years! A great deal of inspiration – and perhaps not a little envy – was felt by those around the world who read in the Army press or watched on video reports of amazing progress. On 26 July 1992, the first anniversary, St Petersburg Corps held a march through the streets. As joyful soldiers followed the flag, martial music from the band compelled other supporters along the way to fall in step. Eight hundred people attended the meeting that morning.

Among those joining the celebration were Ernie and Lily Noyon, a Salvationist couple from L'Islet Corps, Guernsey. Inspired by news of progress in Russia, they had organised a music festival to raise money and had brought the proceeds to St Petersburg themselves. As usual in God's economy, there was a need waiting to be met! A proposal had been approved to appoint a full-time chaplain in a prison for 2,000 inmates to consolidate the ministry of Bible study already being carried out. And here was the chaplain's salary. Ernie and Lily felt a deep bond with the 27 brand-new fellow soldiers and the first local officers – corps sergeant-major, colour sergeant and bandmaster – who were commissioned on the anniversary. During the Second World War The Salvation Army in Guernsey had been forced to close down. The Noyons could share the thrill of rebirth which was being celebrated in St Petersburg.

During the following months links of friendship were forged across national boundaries. Congresses and camps, music campaigns and aid expeditions opened doors for those whose outlook on life changed as they discovered for themselves vast differences – but also central common factors – in lifestyle and expectations.

Norway, still closely involved with the Russian scene, welcomed 50 Russian delegates to its congress in Oslo. John Bjartveit was justly proud to introduce those who had taken the first steps as soldiers under his leadership to his Norwegian colleagues whose practical and prayerful encouragement had been vital. The appearance of these Russians on the streets of Oslo caused a sensation. Fear of the Red Army had hung like a cloud over the city for years, but the sight of the delegation marching along Karl Johan Street in the navy-blue uniform of the respected Salvation Army was wonderful proof of perestroika.

The excitement and colour of Army occasions such as these can sometimes give the superficial impression of a travelling circus. Flags wave, fanfares sound and spotlights play on a rare spectacle in the West – Russian Salvationists! But there is more than spectacle and surprise in these events. When lights have faded and the travellers have departed, there are different memories.

Who would forget the boyish enthusiasm of Vladimir Landyrev, former Red Army officer, saved that March during the visit of General Burrows to Moscow, as he stood before his new General and testified to his new Lord? 'I love Jesus Christ. I love The Salvation Army!' This was no shallow showmanship. Vladimir and his wife, Natasha, were rocks in the foundation of the Army in Russia.

As sensational as the marching Russian Salvationists in Oslo was the appearance of a huge, clean trailer with a foreign registration, winding through narrow, potholed Moscow streets. When it pulled up at steel warehouse gates the guard, although expecting a delivery of supplies, was stunned for a moment to see a real Westerner jump down from the cab with a smile of relief.

The trailer, too, had lasting significance. It was a symbol of Christian co-operation which continued for months. Drivers and volunteer crewmen from Norway, Finland, Sweden, England, arriving in Russia, showed friendly teamwork as they set to, unloading supplies under the direction of Ludmilla before downing the sweet black tea she brewed in her office. Other trailers were driven to Ukraine, Moldova and Georgia. The Army red shield, whatever language it bears, has become a uniting symbol of co-operative concern.

That summer, camps which had been run for Young Pioneers – a highlight for all but the most introvert Russian children – were revived in a Christian context. How children and teenagers from Moscow loved the young Service Corps North Americans and blonde Swedes who came and romped with them. It seemed as if they had stepped straight from the Hollywood movies which were new viewing in Russian homes. They brought gifts, fun, music – but best of all they confirmed the teaching about a loving God which the Russian youngsters received week by week at the corps. Recruits classes were included in the syllabus for a number of young people who were enrolled on the final day.

More than 200 children from St Petersburg took part in day camps with a similar, active programme. Minna Karlström was back from her studies and 30 other members of the corps were mustered to help, resourced with equipment sent by Canadian friends. It was a hectic, happy time – especially for those whose families could not afford to pay for sport, music and cultural activities which had previously been provided free by the Communist Government.

Generous people in other countries were keen to host children for holidays. They showered deprived children with loving attention, but experience showed that this was not the wisest way to help, difficult as it was for people who had never been in Russia to understand. The contrast in living conditions was too great. A better policy was to invite people to help finance camps in Russia itself.

Home league members in Scotland were concerned about the hardships endured by Russian people at this time. They decided to allocate their Helping-Hand Scheme money to assist pensioners who had a miserable existence because they had no family to support them. Not only did the generous Scots promise money, but they also provided a volunteer to set up structured care provision in St Petersburg itself. An experienced, recently-retired professional social worker, Salvationist Betty Moncrieff, knew what she would like to do in the few months she had for the project. Her plan would provide not only care for house-bound elderly people but also paid work for a number of employees – a great benefit.

Arriving in August 1992, she quickly set up home in a typical Russian apartment block and then put her plan to the corps people. It was a great idea! Applicants for the four or five jobs which could be funded were interviewed and the team selected. Anne Sofie Hermo, on service from Norway for a year, was also to be involved.

The work would be simple enough, but Betty trained the carers in methods which would set a standard of excellence. A sense of pride in work done well, which had been almost lost, would make a difference to all those involved in the Home Care scheme. Cleaning materials, scarce at that time, were donated and enquiries were made to locate the most needy members of the community. Every home on the resulting list was visited to assess the need and then each employee was allocated four or five homes to visit each week.

Gradually dark, comfortless rooms were transformed into cosy homes. Shopping and cooking were often part of the service.

Pensioners were encouraged to take an interest in life again as the burden of routine was shared and a pattern of companionship returned to break up long weeks of silence. The glimmer of God's love which had almost been extinguished in their souls glowed again. The myth of Scottish meanness was belied as 'Helping-Hand' pounds were transformed into love and care.

Scottish women were not the only Salvationists and friends who were backing sympathy with hard cash. Recorded or not, the contributions of thousands have enabled the work of the Kingdom in Eastern Europe to progress as it could never have done unaided. A timbrel marathon in Bexleyheath, harvest gifts from Cardiff Grangetown, a 190-mile sponsored walk from the Irish Sea to the North Sea by Manchester divisional staff, not to mention parcels from Penge, support from Safeway, discounts from P&O, Leyland, DAF and BA, human resources from Amoco . . . every act of generosity was of untold value.

Swedish government aid was channelled through The Salvation Army while Melbourne, designated as a 'sister city' to St Petersburg, gave generously. Home league members in New Zealand and USA Central Territory supported the Army's efforts to feed hungry people as well as the children's AIDS clinic in Volgograd, while Irish Salvationists donated a large sum from their carolling appeal. Office supplies, then difficult to obtain in Russia, computers and a vehicle were provided by USA Southern Territory for use at headquarters. Retired officers, who had waited many years for the door to open again to the gospel, gave generously to provide books for cadets, while countless people gave gifts to fill trucks which were driven overland by volunteers who gave time and strength. Practical expressions of love flooded in across the shattered wall of suspicion. It was almost overwhelming.

Chapter 8

COME AND JOIN US!

Leaders are recruited for the growing Army

BY autumn 1992 applications from a number of officers who had responded to the General's appeal for those willing to serve in Russia and the Commonweath of Independent States were being processed. At this stage, most officers working there would be volunteers. Conditions were still such that Army leaders felt the usual procedure of being appointed should not apply. A specific commitment to such work would be the best motivation.

Captain Joseph Smith had developed that commitment during his visit as a member of the social services training team earlier in the year. His wife, Pamela, a teacher by profession, and their small daughter, Francina, would share the adventure. Their task was to consolidate social services in Moscow. They discovered that each officer with an administrative post would also be asked to plant a corps! When candidates had been prepared for officership they would take over leadership of these. Nothing daunted, Joseph and Pamela arrived in the great, grey city on 1 October and began a crash course on survival in the concrete jungle. They were used to cities, but this was something different. They quickly learned the reality of God's provision when normal support structures were not in place.

The evangelist Dr Billy Graham also arrived in Moscow that month. His advent was rather more dramatic than the Smiths' coming but there was a link between the two. Captain and Mrs Ljungholm had been involved in the planning of Crusade '92. The organisers were thrilled when he offered the services of a new corps of Russian Christians. Attractive material for new Christians was studied by soldiers who were to be entrusted with the task of counselling those who decided for Christ. Others were to act as stewards in the huge Luzhniki Stadium.

More than 40,000 people, some with church connections but the majority with no deep knowledge of the Christian faith, filled the stadium as Billy Graham, Cliff Barrow and Joni Eareckson-Tada entered between ranks of uniformed Salvationists. Thousands more stood outside in the cold listening to a relay broadcast. Salvationists Katya Ivanova and Marina Kiralyg were among the team of interpreters, their unruffled demeanour cloaking understandable anxiety. Hundreds came to a spiritual crossroads and chose the way of salvation that night. Many of them were introduced into Christian congregations, including The Salvation Army. Fifty or so elected to become soldiers and joined recruits classes.

During these months contacts had been made with Russian officials who responded with varying degrees of warmth and understanding. Their position was difficult. Many of them had worked satisfactorily, from their point of view, within the old system. Only those who had been allowed to travel outside the Soviet Union and had been perceptive about what they observed and those whose integrity caused them to question things which others quietly swept under the carpet could understand the need for change which foreigners were advocating. The Minister of Social Affairs at this time, Ella Pomphilova, was aware that her ministry needed help to deal with overwhelming social problems. After contact with Sven Ljungholm she stated, 'We can benefit by observing the methods and values employed by The Salvation Army.' While she remained in office Madame Pomphilova helped the Army to navigate through countless bureaucratic channels.

Pioneering work in the two cities had developed in a way few could have envisaged. There were frustrations and difficulties but often these were felt most acutely by expatriate personnel. Russians, used to the lumbering style of bureaucracy and the lack of trust inherited from the past, were on the whole unfazed. *'Eta Rossia!'* – 'That's Russia!' they shrugged with a suggestion of pity for these people who wanted things done yesterday. But strong leadership, Holy Spirit motivation and enthusiasm had worked wonders. Consolidation could now be combined with new initiatives. Leadership changes were put in place to facilitate plans.

Wistfully, John Bjartveit wrote his final report. The 'godchild' of the Norwegian Territory was to be designated a command answering directly to International Headquarters and with its own International Secretary, Colonel Fred Ruth. Commissioner Reinder Schurink, a Dutchman, was to be Officer Commanding from 1 November 1992. A month later Lieut-Colonel Howard Evans, recently-retired principal of the School for Officers Training in the USA Eastern Territory, and his wife, Betty, would arrive to prepare for the first officer-training session. This was planned for the first six months of 1993.

The Bjartveit's next appointment was to Denmark but first they would return home to Norway's Territorial Headquarters to finalise the business with which they had been so involved for two years. The vital role they had played in re-establishing the Army in Russia was recognised by General Eva Burrows in a letter read on her behalf to the large congregation at the farewell meeting at the end of November. 'Your readiness to sacrifice and to face with patience and fortitude the difficulties of these early days of pioneering work is acknowledged by all,' she wrote. With the pain of parents leaving a confident yet immature offspring they said farewell, sure that God would preserve the fruits of their service which they now entrusted to him.

Russians were used to sudden changes in leadership. In the past, the more responsibility people held the more precarious was their position. Yet it was still difficult for them to adjust to the Salvation Army style of international comings and goings. By the end of the year there were officers from the United States, Netherlands and Britain, the majority of whom had little understanding of the Russian language. Most of them came to fulfil a yearning to share the gospel with those who had been deprived of its teaching for so many years.

Captain Mike Olsen and his wife, Ruth, Americans with family roots in the region, had experience in relief work. They arrived to take over much of the administration of the humanitarian aid which was still coming in from the American government. Their large white vehicle emblazoned with the red shield logo soon became a familiar sight on the streets of Moscow. Practically every other vehicle at that time was black or dirty blue!

Not long after the Olsens, two officers with contrasting experiences arrived on the same plane from England in the darkness of a Russian November. Major Gwynneth Evans, another descendent of Karl Larsson, had served in Salvation Army medical work in Ghana, Zimbabwe, Malaysia, Thailand and Japan, where she had held a responsible post in a Tokyo Hospital. She was not relishing the idea of yet another difficult language to learn but felt that she could make some contribution to the Larsson family's unfinished business in her final years of officership. Her appointment was to St Petersburg where she too would combine administration with corps planting.

Her colleague, Major Janet Gilson, had never served overseas – unless you count Northern Ireland! Twenty years service as corps officer, divisional youth secretary and assistant personnel officer at UK Territorial Headquarters, combined with a deep interest in Russia, were her credentials for the appointment of Youth and Candidates' Secretary. She was also to plant a corps in Moscow.

An appeal for officers willing to serve in Russia made during the Southern Territory congress in the United States had nudged Lieut-Colonel James and Mrs Lillian Jay to offer their final years of active

National Health Service Retirement Fellowship (Bromley Branch)

MY LIFE in the Salvation Army by Major Gwyneth Evans, was the topic at the September meeting.

Requiring medical knowledge, Gwyneth qualified as a nurse and midwife in 1960 before travelling to Africa.

She worked with another nurse in a hot, humid five-bed unit for tropical diseases.

It was very difficult because the nearest hospital was 40 miles away and they only had a minibus to transfer patients over muddy or rough roads. Although sometimes this helped to speed up maternity cases.

Gwyneth returned to England to study Japanese, aiming to open a school of nursing in Japan.

She spent years in Malaysia and Zimbabwe as well as three months working in Cambodia's refugee camps.

Her last trip was to Russia, where in 1913 her grandfather set up a Salvation Army centre in St Petersburg.

Gwyneth's welfare work is now with the poor and pensioners in England.

The fellowship meets every third Wednesday of the month at the Education Centre at the Princess Royal University Hospital in Farnborough.

YOUR VIEWS

- Please keep your letters brief
your name, address and a dayt
ters may be edited for space, c
- Views expressed are not thos

Police ma
row is ri

HERE we have a classic example of why this country is going to the dogs. (At Nov 1 at 19

TO THE POINT

HUNG UP ON BILL: I have just checked my itemised telephone bill and found a call I made from my home telephone to a well-known electrical retailer cost me £2.10 for 24 minutes. The number was prefixed 0870. This, according to BT, is a special service rate of 8p per minute. The normal landline charge for an 01 number is 3p per minute, plus connec-

service. Their Texan style and spirit of adventure was certainly needed as they discovered a contrast of climate and living conditions when they arrived in Moscow. The news that he was to be responsible for finance and property in this economic minefield was another challenge for him! His wife was appointed as Commissioner Schurink's English secretary. Her gift of hospitality would be frequently called on as visitors came to share in the exciting experience of a new church in action.

By December the new team was in place. Commissioner Schurink wasted no time in calling them together to work out a strategy, guided by the experience of Captain Ljungholm, now Secretary for Development and Government Affairs. The Commissioner's first shock on his appointment to Russia, which meant leaving much-loved family behind in the Netherlands, had given way to an infectious enthusiasm for what he described as 'the most exciting job in the world'. He would indeed become a 'flying Dutchman', travelling many miles to reconnoitre new ground for planting. Priorities were clear in his mind – as they had been throughout his 46-year ministry. He was here to lead people to Christ.

As they presented Jesus, the commissioner and his fellow officers would need to respect the dignity of the Russian people and value their thousand-year Christian history. To be credible, they would have to be willing to identify with those they came to serve, listening and receiving as well as preaching and giving. They would be called to share the yoke with new Christians, walking with them on equal terms. Only in this way could the great leap forward be made, a leap needed to compensate for years of deprivation.

While these deliberations were taking place, Salvationists and friends in both Moscow and St Petersburg were busy preparing for Christmas. A children's choir was rehearsing intensively for a visit to Sweden and Finland on 8 December. For many years musicians had been among the few people who had been able to travel abroad from the Soviet Union. They became cultural ambassadors for the Soviet way of life. These young Salvation Army musicians had an even greater remit. They were living proof that the ice of persecution and indifference in the Swedes' neighbouring nation was beginning to thaw. During this musical tour the loveliness of their singing and traditional dancing moved their neighbouring friends who had done so much to support them. They were excellent ambassadors.

Undeterred by winter weather, they witnessed in the streets of Stockholm, resplendent in bright blue anoraks. After a hectic tour they returned to Moscow to the kind of busy schedule of carolling familiar to most Salvationists.

Christian festivals in Russia are celebrated according to the Orthodox Church calendar. In the West Christmas pre-dates the Orthodox season by about two weeks. It seemed strange to expatriate staff to be at work when friends and relatives at home were tucking into turkey and plum pudding after carol-playing at the hospital. But this bereft feeling was soon compensated by the wonder of new Christians celebrating joy in their Saviour's birth. Each Army centre was given the choice of which date to keep. In practice, some kept both!

The traditional Christmas children's party in Russia had been like a happy concert. Each organisation – factory, institute, government department – would invite all the children of their staff to its culture palace for a music entertainment. Now few could afford to sustain this programme. Grand halls of culture palaces stood dark and cold, curtains fraying, floodlights dimmed by dust, marble corridors echoing only to the footsteps of the caretaker. If children were invited to such a party they kept their coats on against the cold, and some went away without a bag of gifts.

Here was a way in which the Army could help. Moved by a new awareness of poverty in the country, thousands of people abroad were wanting to add Russian families to their Christmas gift list. Much of this generosity was channelled through The Salvation

Army in Moscow and St Petersburg. Salvationists hired a number of halls, including the prestigious Kremlin Palace of Congresses, for 7 January, and invited music and dance groups to perform. Smartly-uniformed timbrelists added a sparkle and each child went home with a gift. Thousands caught a glimpse of the spirit of Christmas for the first time, adding depth to the normal New Year festivities.

In the deep snow of the countryside a short distance outside Moscow, 150 children linked with the Moscow Corps were at camp with their own leaders and a group of young American Salvationists, which included the daughter of Lieut-Colonel and Mrs Evans, who had come to teach them. Janet Gilson, thrust into preparations for this holiday as soon as she arrived in the country, had quickly discovered that negotiations for premises were full of pitfalls. Days before camp was due to begin, the quoted price for the premises provisionally booked had been increased to an impossible amount. The search began again. On Boxing Day prayer was answered. A good, clean Pioneer camp complex with cooperative staff was secured for a more reasonable rent. The children would not be disappointed. They arrived full of energy on New Year's Day in a temperature of minus 20° centigrade.

Janet soon discovered the tremendous quality of Russian Salvationists in camp situations. At first she doubted her own sanity! Marina Kolkina, her assistant, in effect her 'voice and ears', had a bad dose of flu and could not come to camp, but others, once they understood the aims, shadowed her as she moved about the camp, encouraging, observing. Any suggestion or idea translated to the staff would be met with the response, 'Yes, Major. Don't worry, we'll do it.' And they did. They conjured up fancy dress costumes from next-to-nothing; they comforted small children and controlled older ones; they tramped out in breath-freezing temperatures; they taught Bible truths and pointed the way to Jesus. Natasha and Lydia, Sasha and Vladimir, Misha and Maria, Katya and Irena worked with a will to make the camp a time to remember.

Salvationists in St Petersburg had been just as active. League of mercy members had distributed thousands of gifts in homes, prisons, hospitals and sanatoria. By word and music they made it known that they were God's messengers. They prayed that their listeners would accept the greatest gift of his Son. Hamish Cook, a UK Salvationist, and six friends who were visiting the corps were amazed and inspired by what Geoff and Sandra and their flock achieved.

Santa made a late delivery, by courtesy of British Salvationists. For weeks gifts had poured into the warehouse of the Spa Road Social Services Centre in London. Medical supplies, tinned food, chairs, instruments and music, blankets, winter coats and Bibles were loaded into two 20ft containers. Then there were the shoe-boxes! Individual families had packed them with small, everyday items, tucked in with great ingenuity, and sent them to the Russia Department at IHQ. They kept arriving, to be piled in offices, in corridors, in the basement.

Weeks later, the decorated shoe boxes, some a little battered, brought joy to people far away in dark, one-roomed apartments where such things as bars of soap or pencil and paper were considered luxuries, especially if the breadwinner was in prison or too handicapped to work. From families to families – with much time and thought, driving and carrying, many small miracles were wrought.

Chapter 9

HERALDS OF JESUS

Seventy-five years on . . . a second session of cadets

ONE of the goals resulting from the Army's re-entry into Russia was to devolve leadership to national Salvationists as soon as possible. Pioneers had faith to believe that God had prepared men and women for this responsibility, just as he had selected Moses and Samuel, Peter and Paul to lead his people. Seventy-five years after the first Russian cadets were trained in the then Petrograd, the second group came together in Moscow for a concentrated course of training.

They had already proved themselves in leadership within the corps, in teaching, in witnessing, in serving the neediest people of their community. Interviews with officers confirmed the reality of their calling. Did they understand the full implications of their commitment? Does anyone who answers the call of Jesus? Like any other journey in life, their march behind the Army flag would bring experiences of success and failure, encouragement and disappointment. They had been inspired by the example of the pioneering officers, and they had been obedient to God's call. Only time would tell where this would lead. At the cadets' welcome meeting Cadet Valerie Tateosova sang, 'I'll not turn back whatever it may cost.' Earnest prayers that God would continue to be a bright reality in the lives of these fine men and women burned in hearts moved by her lovely tones.

There was Vladimir Llandyrev, from a Red Army military family, teaching Salvation Army recruits classes as soon as he had signed his own articles of war. Before, he had taught Communist dogma to Russian soldiers. As the son of an officer, he was expected to make his career in the forces. He studied psychiatry, was promoted to the rank of lieutenant-colonel and was slotted into the system. But there was no conviction in his teaching. As cracks began to show in the State his disillusion was confirmed. He needed something more stable in which to put his faith.

His wife, Natasha, was by profession a seismologist who had travelled widely in the USSR recording earth movements. Two teenage boys completed the family. Natasha approached her husband's new interest with some caution but, after 16 years of marriage, she trusted his judgement and supported him. When Commissioner Lindberg and Danielle Strickland visited their home the conversation, Bible reading and prayer they shared increased her understanding and gained her trust. She was happy – radiantly happy – to enter this door of new opportunity.

A younger couple, Philip and Svetlana Rubakov, showed great leadership potential too. For Philip, computers were a huge attraction! He discovered how to use his skills in publicising the Army's activities and producing song sheets and Bible-teaching material. His grasp of English became more fluent, especially during a visit to America, and he was an enthusiastic member of the team. The Rubakovs' first baby was due when the training session began, and the baby's needs had to be remembered in the preparations.

From St Petersburg came Vladimir and Valerie Tateosov, a gifted couple who had much to offer. Vladimir was a psychologist and was a key figure in the prison ministry undertaken by the corps.

Yuri Sidorin came from Presnia. The Christian faith was not new to him and he saw officership as a great challenge which would give him opportunity to bring Christ to his compatriots in a compelling way.

Alexander and Maria Kharkov and their two young boys could have been Salvationists all their lives! Responsibility in civic life had made Alexander wise. His ready smile belied the seriousness of his commitment. The family at that time couldn't communicate easily with their Western colleagues in English but they communicated through a shared love for God and his Kingdom.

Another man with professional qualifications, Yuri Chutkin, completed the group of candidates. He was experienced in legal matters but now he was discovering the part grace played in man's redemption.

Other Salvationists at both corps who showed leadership qualities and spiritual maturity would follow their friends into officer-training in later sessions. The Lord called young and mature, men and women, married and single for service. It was a tremendous responsibility for those entrusted with their training. Some for whom officership was not an option were already giving inspired service as local officers. Their contribution was vital, too.

Training took place in premises sublet to the Army by the Central Baptist Church which had an arrangement with a children's sanatorium to rent one floor of its building, thus providing the doctors with much-needed funds in order to continue their work. Lieut-Colonels Howard and Betty Evans and their assistants from the States, Captains Kellus and Marcia Vanover and Esther Washburn, a volunteer teacher, were pleased with this arrangement which enabled cadets and their children to be resident so that every precious moment of the short session could be utilised.

Everyone involved in training the cadets knew the urgency of the process. Colonel Fred Ruth, on one of his regular visits from London, noted that the 'honeymoon' period of freedom of religious worship was over. 'People do not flock to the meetings in great numbers as they did immediately following the collapse of the Communist government; few are convinced that Christ is their only hope,' he said. The great gust of air which swept through the open door, like the wind of the Spirit at Pentecost, had changed to a gentle, at times almost imperceptible, breeze. There were still many influential people intent on sealing the draught altogether. The Salvation Army in Russia was just a vulnerable seedling, needing every nourishment to help develop firm, deep roots.

A perceptive Russian Christian university lecturer who had suffered for his faith understood the qualities needed for leadership in The Salvation Army. In a letter addressed to General Burrows he wrote, 'I suggest the most difficult issue is the great number of needy people and the problem of motivating and mobilising those who are ready and able to share with their neighbour. . . . The Army must be made attractive to the Russian intelligentsia . . .who have a tradition for humanitarianism. . . . I think officers will need to show all their abilities and talent . . . they will also need God's gift to lead people.' Some of those people were already in the training school.

There were other cities both in Russia and other parts of the Commonwealth of Independent States where civil authorities wanted the Army as a partner in reconstruction, recognising its spiritual impact. Commissioner Schurink and his staff looked eagerly for reinforcements, but they were not arriving in crowds! It was difficult for people to uproot themselves from comfort for the sake of a country which had earned such a bad reputation over the years. Russians were working hard in the established corps but it soon became obvious that a second session of cadets would not be ready by September, as planned. The Heralds of Jesus had a vital task to be good role models.

Training days passed swiftly. Study of the Bible and the doctrines and history of the Army was given deeper meaning through prayer and meditation. Busy involvement in corps life alternated with relaxing social events and domestic chores. The teachers and the taught learned from each other. It was a memorable time for everyone involved.

As June approached, preparations for commissioning were given priority. In any part of the Army world the commissioning of cadets is a highlight but this occasion especially caught interest. General Burrows was coming. There would be visitors from Norway, Switzerland, Britain, Finland, New Zealand and the United States, some of whom were cruising to the city from St Petersburg. All the way from the USA, the Texas Divisional Youth Band was coming to welcome the newest lieutenants with a fanfare. A contingent of unofficial 'soldiers' from Yalta were also to be included and recognised. It was to be a great day.

A strange mixture of excitement and apprehension, familiar to most Salvation Army officers, was felt as 10 cadets made their way to the large cinema palace in central Moscow on 12 June 1993.

First, before becoming the focus of much rejoicing, they had an assignment with their Lord.

In a small room, in the presence of officer colleagues who had guided them to this moment, the 10 Russian cadets responded to the General's words of challenge, by kneeling in turn to sign their covenant to serve God in The Salvation Army. Looking down from panelled walls were large photographs of Communist personalities – men who too had been devoted to a cause – but their structure had crumbled. God was entrusting these 10 men and women to help rebuild on the foundation of his word.

Meanwhile, a large congregation was gathering in the great hall. At three o'clock, prompted by martial music from the Texas Divisional Youth Band, Commissioner Schurink led his General and his cadets into the spotlight. Cameras whirred and clicked. This momentous event would be recalled back home 'down under', across the Atlantic and in many parts of Europe. 'Rejoice, rejoice! Be glad in the Lord and rejoice!' The words sounded out in multilingual song, binding Russian Christians with those who had come far to share their joy.

The cadets recited the Army's articles of faith in Russian before responding with a firm, united *'Da!'* to the challenge voiced by their training principal.

In the quiet beauty of holiness, General Burrows commissioned and ordained Alexander and Maria, Vladimir and Natasha, Philip and Svetlana, Yuri, Vladimir and Valerie, and Yuri. Ten Russian citizens now treasured moments significant to every Salvation Army officer. They were compassed about by a host of witnesses to answered prayer, on earth and in Heaven.

Salvation Army tradition permeates such occasions as this. Vladimir Llandyrev's mother, a uniformed soldier of Moscow Central Corps, proudly received a small silver star, representing mothers of all the new lieutenants. As the wife and mother of senior Red Army officers she was familiar with medals. In fact, because they were so significant to her son, representing his former dogma and values, Vladimir had given his up to Sven Ljungholm when he committed his life to Christ. But this small silver star on a blue background was different. She thanked God that her son and daughter-in-law had caught a new vision for their homeland.

Resplendent in officer's red trimmings and carefully draped sessional flag, Lieutenant Philip Rubakov clearly declared his faith in both Russian and English. Recalling the significance of candles in Russian Orthodox tradition, he acknowledged that he was one of 10 very small lights going out into the darkness. Proof that small lights could be effective in dispelling darkness came in the presence of Lieut-Colonel Alida Bosshardt, 60 years an officer in the Netherlands, honoured by both civic and Army leaders for her work in the dark corners of Amsterdam. As she spoke of her experience it was obvious that her inner strength, goodness, warmth and energy derived from God.

Russian tradition had its moments too. As appointments were announced, long-stemmed roses were brought by soldiers from all parts of the congregation as symbols of love and recognition to the lieutenants. These were their people. Initially they were appointed as understudies to those who had laid foundations, but they were already pastors who understood the nature and language of their flock. Their contribution to the Army's progress was vital.

The evening music festival featuring the Texas youth band and the Moscow Singing Company held a significant surprise. Calling an upright elderly gentleman in Salvation Army uniform to the platform, General Burrows recognised the role of Vladimir Mikhailovich in keeping the spirit of the Army, which he had caught as a teenager in St Petersburg, alive in Yalta for many years. While supporting himself as a labourer he had led a small group in practical ministry to the most needy people in his once prosperous community. Persecuted and imprisoned for his Christian motivation, he was considered an outcast until official attitudes to Christianity became less repressive. Now his redoubtable spirit was honoured as he was presented with the Order of the Founder. William Booth would surely recognise a fellow spirit in Vladimir, who fought for justice almost alone in an alien environment. The presentation of a flag emblazoned with the name of the Yalta Corps which was now to become official and the announcement that Majors Jake and Camie Bender, from USA Central Territory, were to be its corps officers evoked 'Hallelujahs' from the small group who had travelled miles from the Crimea to witness this happy moment.

It is hard to estimate the significance of that weekend in June 1993. Indigenous leadership was a key factor in the vision of those who took the bold step of leading The Salvation Army into Russsia. The training, so brief, would now be put to the test. These Heralds of Jesus were eager to proclaim his message and to set the pattern for those who would follow them into officership.

Chapter 10

OUT IN THE FIELD

Pastoring the growing flock

DOORS of opportunity for effective work were now ajar in many places. The new lieutenants and their colleagues from overseas were eager to enter although, like the apostle Paul, they knew that there would be those who opposed them.

At this time (1993) there were five corps in Moscow, three in St Petersburg, including Pushkin, and one in Kiev, the capital of Ukraine. New work was commencing in Volgograd, Yalta and Tblisi, Georgia's capital. At least 10 other cities had responded favourably to approaches made by Captain Mike Olsen who was working to implement the expansion plan formed at the beginning of the year. Given suitable personnel and adequate finance it seemed there was no limit to what could be achieved. Even with severe limitations in both of these resources, almost unbelievable progress was being made. The process compared with the early days of the Army in Britain, when corps were created by the fire of enthusiasm of people in neighbouring districts who had found new hope in the gospel message.

How can this dynamic process be conveyed in cold print? The faithfulness, inspiration, trials and achievements of hundreds whose contribution to the whole has been vital can only be glimpsed. Soldiers ministering to patients in hospital, musicians proclaiming the gospel in crowded cities or small meeting places, interpreters giving voice to the messages of reinforcement personnel, local officers carrying responsibility, teachers, writers, home league members – the commander and his staff have no function without them. They are the light and salt of the Kingdom of God.

A spark was lit in Lydia's life when she met The Salvation Army in Moscow in 1992. Like many older Russian people who had worked for the good of the nation for many years she was distressed by the state the country had disintegrated into. Many of her suburban apartment-block neighbours were living in great poverty. Each time she travelled in the city she was aware of people who were even more desperate, without identity because they lacked official papers and so without a home. Some had been signed out of hospitals or prisons with no support. Children grown too old for orphanages joined dissolute no-hopers in derelict buildings, begging and stealing for a living. There was little one woman could do but be thoughtful for her own neighbours.

The press, considerably changed in recent months, reported new movements which were appearing. Among these was The Salvation Army, a philanthropic international Christian church. Lydia decided to go to the meeting she saw advertised.

The hall was crowded with Russians who, like herself, had come out of curiosity. On the platform were a tall American man and his wife in dark, military-style uniforms. Young Russian students interpreted their words. The religious nature of the meeting was obvious, although it was very different from Orthodox worship. Simple Christian songs, prayers and verses read from the Bible were interspersed with information about this new group and short talks by a number of Russians about their personal Christian faith. The motive behind the social work Lydia had read about was becoming clear. These people followed the example of Jesus by caring for the outcast and serving their neighbour. As children of God, they saw all people as their responsibility.

During conversation after the meeting Lydia asked if there was any way in which she could help. There certainly was! People attending the Army were being enlisted to serve meals to pensioners in more than 20 *stolovars* which were supplied with food through the Army. The following week she went to the address she had been given, donned a red apron emblazoned with the Army shield, and set to work.

Lydia was moved by these experiences like her fellow seeker, journalist Svetlana, who wrote: 'The Army has taken helpful aspects of military life – discipline, loyalty, organised structure – and used them to serve weak, disadvantaged people in society. When such people have regained their self-respect they are ready to listen to the good news that God's grace is available to all. This is the power and the motivation of The Salvation Army.'

Continuing to attend meetings, before long Lydia made her way to the front of the stage after the Captain's invitation to follow Jesus Christ. Careful teaching about the implications of her decision in following weeks confirmed feelings into faith. With God's blessing she could help to bring relief to suffering people by becoming a soldier in this Army. She studied the Bible eagerly, and began to pattern her life on the teaching she found in its pages. Lydia was one of the first group of 65 senior soldiers in Moscow enrolled by General Burrows in March 1992.

Travelling back to the suburb of Lublino each evening, she dreamed of the day when The Salvation Army would work in her own district. It needed both the practical help and the spiritual influence which the Army would bring.

Not long after Lydia's enrolment a planning meeting took place which was to transform her dream into reality. In addition to Moscow Central and Presnia corps, recently opened by Captain and Mrs Olsen, new corps were to be planted in a number of other suburbs of Moscow: Babushkino, Sokolniki and . . . Lublino. In addition to responsibility for candidates and youth work in Moscow, Major Janet Gilson was to be Lublino's first corps officer.

A large building had already been earmarked, but a contract for its use had yet to be negotiated.

Within days of arriving in Russia, Janet was driven out to survey the 'field' of Lublino. There was not a blade of grass to be seen. Grey predominated. Her return walk to the metro station alone became a prayer walk. She prayed for the elderly, lonely people behind the rows and rows of windows which seemed to stare suspiciously at her; for the children who were trudging back from school; for the men who lounged in the yards, workless since the car production plants which dominated the area had closed down; for the drab women lugging precious potatoes back from market, wishing they had more to put on the meal table. Lydia was right. Lublino needed care.

The experience of planting a totally new corps was daunting. Methods used initially in Russia of hiring a large hall and inviting people through the press were unlikely to have the same response in this depressed, out-of-town area. Besides, this procedure was costly and the 'satellite' corps were to run on a very tight budget and lots of faith!

Ludmilla, at the warehouse, heard about the venture. 'Why not use a *stolovar*?' she suggested. 'There's one in the Lublino district.' The supervisor was happy to give an hour's extra time each Thursday evening to keep it open. After all, she would have been out of work long ago had the Army not provided food for her customers. The English woman and her Russian helpers seemed genuine. So leaflets announcing a children's Christian club were distributed in apartment blocks and at school gates.

The first club meeting at Lublino took place on 20 November 1992. Major Gilson, with her translator, Marina, and Natasha, an experienced young people's leader from Moscow Central Corps, prayed that God would bless their efforts and then waited! To their delight, 27 children made their way to the *stolovar* that evening. Nine of their mothers wanted to stay as well, eager to share in this new experience. Shyness was shed along with heavy outdoor

95

garments as Natasha coaxed the children to join in some lively games. This was fun!

After a drink and a bun, chairs were drawn into a circle and the children were introduced to Jesus. The bouncy young woman who had played with them was now serious. Drawn by her lively face, toddlers and teenagers listened intently. Who knows what passed through their minds as they heard about the God whose Son had been a child like them, playing and learning. They heard that as a man, Jesus had treated children with love and respect. Children are cherished in Russian society. Mothers, seated at the canteen tables, out of the way, listened and approved. They would bring the children again next week.

Lydia heard about the club the following Sunday as she chatted with friends while serving tea after the meeting at Central Corps. Great news! She must offer to help.

The club continued to draw new children and their mothers. Ten of them were among the 200 or so children and leaders who went to the Army's New Year camp in the country. It was a time they wouldn't have missed, with a grand climax on Orthodox Christmas Day, celebrating the birth of Jesus at a great concert party back in the city.

Disappointment came in the New Year when negotiations for the proposed building for Lublino Corps proved fruitless. But this was a continuing problem. The new nation was still very unsettled. Renting accommodation to strange religious groups was risky. Central Corps was continually forced to find new premises – seven in the first two years – and St Petersburg Salvationists had similar problems. The Culture Palace which had been approached was now home to a Baptist congregation, a safer option for the owners. It was disappointing, but at least there would be a Christian influence in that part of the region. Perhaps it would be better to look for somewhere nearer the *stolovar* anyway. Meanwhile, the club was Lublino Corps, but the vision was far greater than a weekly meeting for children and their mothers.

Having visited a number of schools to talk about the Army, Janet had wondered if it would be feasible for the corps to share school premises. There was a small, old school not far from the *stolovar*. 'It's possible, Major,' said Marina when the idea was mooted. So they spoke to the director and, to their delight, he was interested, and showed them round the school. There was a small hall, with a piano, on the first floor, and a room downstairs which would store food and clothes for distribution.

Now it is one thing to make a verbal agreement, and quite another to make a contract and begin a programme. The process, which felt like a hurdle race for horses, took about six weeks. One hurdle, the prefect (head of the local authority) approved; another, Svetlana and Irina were employed to run a 'charity shop', distributing food and clothing to 210 families listed by the local social workers; then, a tricky one, long negotiations about rent were concluded satisfactorily; finally, during the canter to the opening day, open-air meetings were held in the snow.

Young Salvationists from Moscow Central and Presnia were proud to help the fledgling corps. They sang the gospel message and gave out invitations to the first meeting. Already Lydia's Christian witness had been noticed by her neighbours. Now, transferring from Central Corps where she had been nurtured in the faith, she could help them to make the same discoveries and share the same companionship.

Not everyone welcomed The Salvation Army to Lublino. During the first evening session of Christian teaching four windows were smashed and stones hurled into the director's office. The Devil had his troops! Undeterred, on Sunday morning teenagers from the club helped to transform the small, dismal schoolroom into a place of worship, not an ornate shrine, but a typical Salvation Army hall with flag, mercy seat and a warm welcome. In the first congregation which crowded the room adults were outnumbered by children. At the end of the meeting, in response to the invitation to respond to God's love, two youngsters knelt at the mercy seat. 'I believe for Lublino!' wrote the corps officer in her diary that day.

Good news spread quickly through the community and many came for help when clothes and food were distributed from the small store at the school. In addition, free hot meals were provided for the children at the *stolovar* before Thursday club. A programme of Christian teaching and another children's club at the school complemented Sunday meetings. The premises were not ideal, but it was obvious that the Army was beginning to take root in Lublino. People were finding Christ and learning to serve in turn. Visiting her people in their homes helped Major Janet Gilson to understand the quiet dignity of their lives. They did not have all the conveniences found in most Western homes but they were careful housekeepers and generous hosts. She also discovered great need, particularly where large families, some with an absent father, struggled to exist on next to nothing.

By midsummer the Army was well-established in the community. When the first adult seekers knelt at the mercy seat on the first Sunday in June, their few paces to the front of the hall represented a great step forward in the progress of the corps. A few days later, Lieutenants Vladimir and Natasha Llandyrev were commissioned and appointed to the corps. Lydia felt that Lublino's lean months were over. She believed that Vladimir and Natasha, who she knew well from the days when they worshipped together at Moscow Central, and Janet, who she had begun to trust, would work well together to build on the foundations already laid.

The joy of having Russian officers as partners was almost indescribable. Janet had watched them transform through the months of training into people who were spiritually awake to the gospel and convicted of their calling. Soon there would be no need for tedious translation of the gospel message. It would ring out with power in the language of the people.

It had become obvious that the shabby school premises were no longer suitable for a growing corps. Searching the district, the officers discovered a larger school, tucked away behind tall apartment blocks. The director, having heard of the impact The Salvation Army made on a community, was happy to negotiate a contract. The large school hall could be used on Sundays. A small room near the entrance would be set aside for an office and classrooms would be available when needed. Before long the prefect of the district, whose grandson had been attending the Army Sunday school, had sanctioned the arrangement, a very reasonable rent was agreed, the contract signed and keys handed over. The only fear was that elderly people and children would not travel to the new premises although they were not far from the old school. As it happened, four mothers, who later became soldiers, and their children happily made the move. The future of others had to be prayerfully placed in God's hands.

Holidays, a busy programme of camps run by the Army, making their presence known in the new area, and preparing their young people for an adventurous journey by coach to Amsterdam with Major Janet Gilson for an international youth congress, occupied Lublino's officers during the summer months. On Sundays Vladimir would take the brand-new Army flag and walk around the streets, stand outside shops and beside bus stops, telling anyone who would listen about the Lord and his representatives who had come to serve them. When others joined him for open-air meetings, many people paused to listen and ask questions. The good news spread quickly.

In the autumn the enlarged corps programme burst into action. In addition to Lydia, Yuri and Larissa Makarov and their daughter, Marina, transferred from Presnia Corps to add to the team of workers.

Long before the Army had officially returned to Russia, Yuri Makarov's life had been changed by reading the Bible, which had already begun to be more accessible. Its inspired insight to life's problems and common-sense code of conduct appealed to Yuri and his wife, Larissa. Although they were not linked with a church, they became Christians. Until the Billy Graham Crusade which they attended in Moscow, Yuri and Larissa knew nothing about The Salvation Army, but they were impressed by the deportment of Salvationists who ushered worshippers to their seats and later counselled those who sought spiritual guidance. The idea of wearing uniform to be identified as Christian soldiers appealed to them too.

Since becoming Christians they had felt a growing need to belong to a church. This introduction was an answer to prayer. The Makarovs were among those who, guided by leaflets given out as part of the Graham campaign, found their way to Presnia Corps, attended recruits' classes and stood beneath the Army flag in uniform to be sworn in as soldiers. Increasingly they became aware that the Movement, which helped people to grow spiritually and cared for their physical needs, could make a great contribution in their country, where the Church was often perceived as elitist and inward-looking.

Watching Yuri, Larissa and Marina taking their place with Lydia and the officers in the school hall, following their transfer from Presnia, it would seem that they had been lifelong Salvationists! They became involved in teaching and training both children and adults. Larissa's main role was to manage a home-care programme, patterned on the work pioneered by Betty Moncrieff in St Petersburg. She interviewed and employed a team of men and women and together they worked out ways of offering support to elderly and disabled people in their homes. The most isolated people, who were identified from a list obtained from the prefect's office, were visited by Larissa. She assessed their needs and appointed a key-worker. Soon 10 homes every week were brightened by the influence of kindness and concern. Later the expanded service regularly reached 25 lonely people.

Hospital conditions had deteriorated severely in recent years. Another of Larissa's projects was to offer support in the district hospital. Again, the ministry was practical as well as spiritual. In the week corps people cleaned and scrubbed. On Sundays their music rang along corridors and cheered uncomfortable patients and overworked staff. Two of the staff, warmed by what they saw, went to the corps and in time became soldiers.

It was impossible to solve every human problem but they did what they could. In one room lay a young man in a desperate state. Visiting Moscow from another CIS state, he had been involved in a scuffle on a mainline station, falling in front of a train. His terrible injuries resulted in the amputation of both legs and an arm. He had no friends or relatives. What could be done for him?

In a flurry of activity a number of things were done. Clothes were purchased – he had nothing but shapeless hospital gowns – and ingeniously adapted to be smart yet practical; the complex process of obtaining papers which would enable him to be repatriated was begun and, best of all from his immediate point of view, he discovered a Walkman and a number of popular tapes wrapped in the package which his visitors brought. He was delighted! Now there was a gleam of hope in his shattered life.

People in the vicinity of School Number 1143, Lublino Region, had many surprises in the autumn of 1993. Salvationists were given curious glances as they moved in and out of the office. Glances changed to stares of amazement when people realised that some of the strangers spoke English. They got to know that the ones with red trimmings were the leaders and would sometimes stop them and ask questions. Quite a number of the children began to join in the Army's activities.

Attempts to revive the children's club at the *stolovar* after the usual summer decline didn't succeed. The club had lost its impetus now that the main focus of the corps was some distance away. Eventually it closed, acknowledging that even in God's economy things appear to fail as well as succeed. In Russia, as anywhere, this lesson had often to be learned – but it is never easy to accept.

The country's economy was still plagued with rapid inflation. Every rouble counted. Next day, it counted for less. Officers, particularly Russian, found that personal financial worries were adding to the stress. Food aid from the West was still available for distribution. People in Lublino needed it, so the school director was approached. Was there anywhere the Army could use as storage?

Key in hand, the director led the officers to a short flight of steps at the back of the building and unlocked a door at the bottom. Switching on the lights of the underground room she said, 'Would this do?' In unison, Vladimir, Natasha and Janet said, '*Da!*'

They saw a long, narrow, dry area, lights shielded with metal, leading off a small entrance hall with a locked sideroom. Down here, in Communist times, every 14-year-old had been taught to shoot. Another Army would now use it to store ammunition in the war against want. Swords into ploughshares indeed!

Thus school staff and Salvationists coexisted in increasing understanding to everyone's benefit. Schoolboys eagerly hurried to help unload lorries, teachers appreciated the positive atmosphere, canteen staff happily worked overtime to provide food for special occasions and Salvationists valued the privilege of sharing such good facilities in the heart of a bustling community. These conditions helped a great deal to establish and develop the corps.

During these months Janet Gilson had been increasingly busy with her other responsibilities at Command Headquarters. Local officer leadership training courses had taken place in Moscow and St Petersburg, planned as a way of developing potential leaders to compensate for the postponement of the second session of officer-training. Many soldiers, including some from Lublino, too old to become cadets but eager to learn more about taking responsibility in the Army, benefited from these days of study. Those who taught them were thrilled to see them develop both within their own corps and in new initiatives.

Meanwhile, Janet was keeping a steadying, guiding watch over the Lublino flock with its devoted Russian shepherds. Her regular meetings for prayer and planning with the Llandyrevs identified problems, which were tackled together, and confirmed that when the time came for them to take full responsibility the corps would be in good hands. The past year had been the most challenging and fulfilling of her officership and the moving-on process would not be easy. Before this happened, though, there would be more exciting things afoot.

The enrolment of the first men and women, boys and girls to have found their faith at Lublino took place on 21 November 1993. By 10.30 am the new snow on the school playground was imprinted by many tracks which met at the front steps. Inside there was a hubbub. Young and old crowded up the stairs and soon filled the rickety seats in the hall, hushed now by the presence of children in a circle of prayer at the end of Sunday school.

The office was overflowing as more than a dozen new soldiers were checked for smartness by Natasha and Lydia. Satisfied that uniform hats and junior soldier ties were properly adjusted, they took their places on the front rows. The arrival of Commissioner Schurink, proud to enrol his new soldiers, and Lena, his translator, added to the sense of occasion. It was a day of great rejoicing and gratitude to God.

Lydia, corps hostess par excellence, had the samovar boiling at the end of the meeting and the new soldiers were welcomed with a feast – a miracle in itself. Friends from Moscow Central Corps shared her sense of fulfilment. They missed her contribution and fellowship. The Central Corps pianist, Vladimir Kolyenko, who was often 'on loan' helping the new corps to become established, created another link between corps. Yuri and Larissa's friends from their first spiritual home, Presnia Corps, supported too. In the true spirit of church growth they were thrilled to see that the new branch was bearing fruit. They were learning that sacrifice is never in vain in God's Kingdom.

The corps in the school became a haven of warmth and love which attracted more and more people.

On Sundays they were drawn by the music, the friendship, the novelty and above all by the word of God expounded with relevance, humour, challenge and comfort by Lieutenants Vladimir and Natasha Llandyrev. In a suburban school hall often decorated with childish motifs, and without incense or icons, the depth of Russian spirituality was felt as soon as the Bible was opened or when worshippers were invited to pray.

'Move, Holy Spirit, move in my life. . . .' The chorus was often sung by that congregation, and the prayer was usually answered immediately as a quiet, purposeful group knelt in prayer at the mercy seat. Identifying with these seekers, friends knelt or stood by them. Sensitively, they would be led into a deeper experience of God in the coming days.

The lieutenants were always busy after the meeting, noting need, cheering the sad, encouraging newcomers. There would be plenty for their willing team of workers to do the following week. The responsibility of distributing food and clothing to the community was taken seriously. The most needy families, identified through the local social services, were given priority. Lydia and her friends would inform them by telephone of the time to come to the school underground warehouse to collect rations which were welcomed as a valuable addition to the kitchen cupboard. Others would be given a share as long as stocks lasted.

Clothing was distributed with equal care. News soon went round the neighbourhood when a delivery was made and people waited eagerly for a phone call – every home had been supplied with phones by the Communist regime. To prevent reselling on a large scale, each person was rationed to three garments. Russian mothers, keen for their children to look smart, selected carefully from the sorted clothing and they were thrilled if they found an outfit for themselves as a bonus.

Celebrating the first Christian festival as a corps family was a great highlight. A drama student eagerly transformed the Christmas story into a play for the children to enact and carols, virtually unknown before, were excitedly learnt. Invitations to a concert party were sent to the director of the school. On 25 December, a normal working day for Russians, children packed the hall, pleased with this change of routine. As a spotlight followed 'Joseph and Mary' down the school hall they watched in wonder. This was different from the usual winter celebrations with the visit of Grandfather Frost and his snow maidens. This scene was about workmen and housewives. True, kings and angels put in an appearance as well. It was quite puzzling to the onlookers but there was a sense of peace and joy about it all. Ideas they had been given that Christianity was all nonsense were dispelled in the minds of some of the children. They determined to go again and discover more.

That evening Lydia and other soldiers and recruits crowded into Janet's apartment for a more intimate celebration. As she looked at the thoughtful, candlelit faces of her friends she mused about the way God had worked in their lives. She was proud to feel Russian. She was thrilled that the Light of all nations had come to dispel the frozen wastes of this country. But she was aware of dark shadows, too. The elemental forces of good and evil would continue the struggle to gain control of Russia's soul.

The good influence in Lublino was much in evidence at the Christmas Sunday meeting next day. A packed congregation included the prefect of the district and the school director. The newly-installed General Secretary, American Colonel Milford Hickam, and his wife Patricia, enrolled six senior and eight junior soldiers. The new soldiers were especially welcome as two of Lublino's soldiers, Yuri and Larissa, were entering the training college in the new year.

The Llandyrevs led their people into an exciting and busy year. Every time Janet Gilson returned from visiting distant parts of the command where doors were opening, she praised God for the way his Spirit was moving in the corps. What a privilege it was to be involved! She coveted closer links with her flock which the language barrier and other responsibilities prevented but she rejoiced to see that Vladimir and Natasha were totally committed to the people and the neighbourhood.

It was now time to commission local officers – corps sergeant-major, treasurer, secretary, home league secretary, league of mercy secretary, young people's workers and songster leader. The basic programme was like that of Salvation Army corps around the world: a worshipping, learning group with a practical and moral influence in the wider community. Where appropriate, adjustments were made to suit specific conditions and legal requirements.

Corps Sergeant-Major Nina took over responsibility for the Home Care programme when Larissa became a cadet. A training visit to America gave Nina new impetus and vision. Her team worked well, matching their service to the individual needs of their clients, each of whom was made to feel extra special on their birthday. Children from the corps visited with Home Care staff and entertained with song and drama, presenting a gift. Traditional flowers and chocolate were often replaced by something more practical – home-made bedlinen, a dustpan and brush and even a kitten were among things received with a big smile! A meals-on-wheels service was one of Nina's dreams. Meanwhile, she provided the only alternative they could manage – food-on-feet! When visiting each person she added comforting words and prayers to her bright conversation and observation of need.

An insight into the international Army world always gave Lydia a thrill. She had never been taught English and was reticent to join the English conversation class which was held at the corps, but she communicated through hospitality and kindness. A visitor from overseas, be it commissioner or corps cadet, was treated as a VIP. Even those who were fellow soldiers of the corps, such as the British songster-leader, were never without the offer of a helping hand with heavy garments or a hot drink when coming in from the cold. The Sydney Staff Songsters became friends within minutes of coming to Lublino in the course of their Russian tour. It was great to have the freedom of international links after so long in isolation.

Another lesson to learn was that Salvationists understand giving to be part of their service to God. When Command Headquarters issued information about the international annual appeal for funds, the local officers were keen to give everyone, even pensioners, an opportunity to take part. The appeal was launched well before the date of the altar service and week by week soldiers and friends of the corps came early and queued to deposit roubles they had put aside. Natasha Llandyrev and the treasurer carefully listed the donations and the week before the offering gave each person a paper noting their total amount to put into the special envelopes which had been supplied. The resulting sum was an indication that people were learning the joy, as well as the responsibility, of giving to God.

Under Natasha's guidance, young people of the corps were taking an increasing part in teaching the children, preparing visual aids and making the Bible come alive. Timbrel playing was popular. Luba and Marina patiently taught the younger girls routines they themselves had learnt at camp. Worship dance was another means of communicating their faith in moments of praise and prayer.

They were encouraged to make friends with their contemporaries from other corps in regional and command youth events. Lublino was well-represented at residential youth councils. In the summer they made friends with American Service Corps team members and decided that they would like to be involved in such a team some time soon. Summer camps went with a swing, and then many families escaped the heat of Moscow and went off to the country. Many of those who attended the corps were too elderly to travel or had no dacha to retreat to so the corps programme continued, with outings to the country added now and then. Even when the Llandyrevs had their holiday, local officers and cadets made sure that nothing was neglected.

Of course, the corps was not immune to problems of clashing personalities, awkward officials, discouragement and conflicting interests. A few of the soldiers who had stood sincerely beneath the flag at their enrolment had strayed. Other religious groups with bright attractions were active in the district and had caused confusion. The pastors had to seek the lost and comfort the sick, while ensuring that those still within the flock were nourished into maturity.

Always looking for projects to involve people in Christian ministry, Vladimir and Natasha Llandyrev arranged for a group of young people to be taken to Ekaterinburg, far away on the edge of the Ural mountains, where Major Cynthia Shellenburger and Captain Glenda Daddow were pioneering Salvation Army work. It was a New Year visit and Christmas celebrations would be included. It was a great adventure!

Several adults and a dozen teenagers journeyed by train two days and nights. That in itself was a witness as the Christmas message was heard down the corridor when impromptu singing rehearsals took place! Evening prayers were quietly said in a compartment as the train chugged on through the dark winter's night.

The youngsters from Lublino worked in partnership with the Ekaterinburg people, distributing gospel leaflets and visiting a children's home where they gave gifts and acted the traditional Russian story of Babushka, the old woman who was so pre-occupied with daily chores that she missed the opportunity to see the child Jesus.

On New Year's Day arrangements had been made for the group to take part in a concert party for veterans. The year was 1995, half a century since the Second World War ended, and veterans were to be honoured all over Russia. The Lublino youngsters were excited. Natasha was nervous –would they concentrate? She was anxious that they would be good representatives of the Army and, above all, of God, so that the small group of Salvationists in the city would be respected and encouraged.

There was a great crowd of lively, elderly people in the concert hall, many wearing medals and carrying flowers. Professional performers took their turns on stage, and were applauded enthusiastically. Now it was time for Natasha to lead her smartly-uniformed group forward. The young people sang like angels! Then Natasha, standing poised and purposeful in the spotlight with Bible in hand, spoke simply of the gospel message and The Salvation Army which had come to serve the people of the city. Guitar notes broke the silence after she had spoken and Mousha and Dennis sang of God's love to the hushed audience.

Many questions were asked and information given, invitations spoken as the audience dispersed. It was great to see some of them at the Army next day, when they witnessed the enrolment of the first three soldiers of Ekaterinburg Corps.

A special bond between the two corps was forged that weekend. Conditions in Ekaterinburg were not easy and eventually the Army had to withdraw from the city, but those who had sown the seed of the gospel message trusted God to use their efforts to extend his Kingdom.

So seasons passed, rain and sunshine, growth and decline, in the corps in School No 1143. Other soldiers went to be trained as officers. New people grew spiritually and took over their responsibilities. Outposts were established at Marino and Pechatniki, the first becoming a corps with its own Russian lieutenant. The Orthodox Church authorities in the Pechatniki district were at first resentful, but relationships improved so much that sometimes the lieutenant and the Orthodox priest went together to visit patients in hospital. Lydia and her friends worked ceaselessly and the whole region of Lublino felt their influence.

By now there were growing Salvation Army corps in many other places, each with their own pattern of development. Every pastor had a different vision and skills but all were dedicated to the command of Jesus: 'Feed my lambs . . . care for my sheep.'

Chapter 11

INASMUCH

Salvationists find avenues of social service

THINK back to the collapse of Communism, when hidden nations were revealed to the outside world. After the euphoria came pity. Pictures of stark poverty and hopelessness filled newspapers and television screens – hollow-eyed street children; workless, hopeless men; destitute families and dignified elderly people living in comfortless, dark rooms; doctors struggling to heal without resources; politicians stunned by people-power. 'Something must be done!' cried those who became almost ashamed of their affluence. Compassion in action followed. The Church, particularly proactive denominations like The Salvation Army, was urged to be involved.

Tension between spiritual and social ministry is always present in the Church, as it was in the reactions to Christ's own ministry. Priest and scribe criticised his caring, especially when it increased his popularity with the crowds or was for those they branded 'sinners' and so deserved to suffer. It is understandable if dispirited churchmen react in a similar way today.

Twentieth-century politicians and economists also had doubts about the long-term value of humanitarian gifts. An article in *The Financial Times* of 12 February 1992 headed, 'Russia tangled in politics of aid', pointed out the downside of European Economic

Community policies. Many people benefited in the short term but repercussions in domestic trade could be detrimental to the growth of the Russian economy.

Besides, the very fact that the collapse of the structure, purported to be the strongest in the world, had taken place in full view of intrusive cameras and had been relayed across the globe was an immense blow to national pride. That dependency can diminish human beings also needed to be reckoned with.

The strong social conscience of The Salvation Army is well-known, but its spiritual wellspring is not always understood. It was vital that the right balance be achieved in countries which had long been officially atheist yet had a strong, if dormant, church. When initial plans for the Army's re-entry into Russia and other socialist states were being considered, its leaders made a conscious decision not to become heavily engaged in social work, to the detriment of its prime purpose – healing the wounded soul of these nations in the name of Christ. In practice, it was difficult to keep a balance. William Booth recognised that evangelists in the slums of London needed a different approach to those in genteel Gloucester and wealthy Windsor. A starving man cannot be expected to be hungering after righteousness. A sensitive Christian's first instinct is to feed him, but his responsibility does not end there. Even more vital in eternal values is the offer of salvation.

The soul of Russia was starving. People were craving spiritual food which Salvationists were ready to share but there were great expectations of practical help too, perhaps more by people who wanted to give, than from those in need. The end of the Gulf War, mercifully sooner than expected, left a mountain of unwanted food. Generous bureaucrats, sympathetic to their old enemy's plight, yet still wary of its integrity, decided that the food should be given to Russian citizens but that an internationally recognised organisation, The Salvation Army, should be responsible for its distribution. It was a commission the Army could scarcely refuse, although it would make great demands on limited resources.

So at the beginning of 1992 boxes and boxes of 'Desert Storm' supplies were trucked in, adding to overseas aid already available to the Army. Government grants from the United States 'Food for Peace' scheme paid for warehousing and transport, and Captain Mike Olsen devised procedures for distributing the goods as fairly as possible. Residential homes for children and elderly people, support groups for the disabled and chronically sick, *stolovars* and soup-runs were supplied. Much of the food was unfamiliar to Russian palates – and cooking instructions were totally incomprehensible – but any addition to the store cupboard was welcome.

Dozens of Russian Salvationists and friends became involved in this vast operation. In a society where the idea of personal responsibility for a needy neighbour had been replaced by a cold State system, this experience was new but they soon learnt the pleasures of service with a smile. Many quickly understood the Christian motive, developed a compassionate spirit and became key-workers as each corps developed its own social programme.

Lieutenants Geoff and Sandra Ryan, grounding their St Petersburg flock in Christian faith and practice, began to develop a social outreach complementing the larger projects undertaken by the Ljungholms. First they established a weekly feeding programme. Nine teams of volunteers, each with a uniformed Salvationist, collected soup, purchased from a local restaurant, in large military-style vacuum flasks from Norway. They took soup to a number of housebound people whose names were supplied by a charitable association. The simple action meant a lot to those who had little to bring them joy.

Regular hospital ministry was arranged. In the weeks prior to Christmas, corps people packed about 2,000 'sunshine bags' for children in hospital. They received them after watching a puppet show and listening to the story of the first Christmas illustrated by flannelgraph.

Those who were isolated by wrongdoing rather than sickness were not neglected. Opportunity for Bible study within prison walls was provided and appreciated by many. Eventually a Salvation Army chaplain was appointed and given facilities in Colony No 6, where 1,500 men were imprisoned. Christian books, food and clothing were distributed. Those nearing the end of their sentences were assured that the Army would continue to offer support as they adjusted to life in the changed world outside.

Each of these projects was undertaken prayerfully, resisting the temptation to make Christianity 'doing' rather than 'being'. 'Almost daily we have to turn down opportunities that any officer would welcome anywhere else,' wrote Geoff. He and Sandra applied the brake when necessary to keep a good balance between spiritual and social activity. They wanted to be sure that service sprang from love, not duty.

When the Army returned to Russia's capital there were very visible scars of human suffering on the streets of Moscow, especially near the once-grand railway stations from which lines stretched across the former USSR. Sadly, similar effects of alcohol dependence and despair are found in most of the world's large cities, and in many places The Salvation Army identifies with people whose home is the pavement. Russians are not proud of such conditions but they often shrugged them off as normal and left unsympathetic officials to deal with the problem when it became acute. The first Salvationists, consciences awakened, saw beneath the dirt and bruises and followed the lead of officers who took out Army vehicles with food and clothing for those whom most people despised.

Following his lecture tour, Captain Joseph Smith returned to Russia with his wife and daughter, appointed to co-ordinate social services in Moscow and to plant Sokolniki Corps. They came because they believed that, as Hosea had prophesied to his own nation, the valley of trouble could become a door of hope (see Hosea 2:15).

Recruiting paid staff and volunteers, Joseph developed the weekly soup run to a daily service. It was difficult to extend this work in the open streets without the glare of publicity which naturally displeased and embarrassed the authorities. They became less tolerant towards those who drifted into station premises. The Army was asked to move to corners out of sight of the travelling public.

Major Ivy Nash, arriving to work with Joseph, was stunned by what she saw in the streets, in spite of long experience in inner-city corps in Britain. Angered by the apparent indifference on the part of city authorities she battled to gain facilities where homeless people could wash and rest for a while in safety. She gained respect and co-operation in some places but far too often she met closed doors. Most Russians held the opinion that facilities for people who deserved help were adequate. The rest were not worth bothering about.

Supported financially by many friends who were moved by Ivy's touching accounts of her experiences, she worked on serving soup on icy station forecourts with a team of helpers, and befriending vagrant families who made makeshift homes in huge station waiting rooms, the staff turning a blind eye.

Sokolniki Corps was gradually building a body of fine Christians who added to the workforce. Oleg, aged 17, was converted during the Billy Graham campaign in 1992. His mother, Nadeshda (whose name means 'hope'), was also a Salvationist. When Oleg's 19-year-old brother was killed in the Afghan war Nadeshda formed a national support group for other mothers bereaved by the war. Attracted by the opportunity to put his new faith into action, Oleg offered to help with the soup run. Not only did this young Russian break bread to give to the hungry but he could also speak to them and share his faith.

Another key person in the team was Sasha, a remarkable young man. Incompetent surgery after a childhood accident left him paralysed from the waist down. Defying expectations, he taught himself to move on crutches, enrolled for an advanced language course and graduated. He was enrolled by General Burrows in

March 1992 and transferred to Sokolniki Corps when it opened, throwing himself wholeheartedly into the activity. Bible study, worship, station ministry, prison visitation, *Vestnik* selling . . . Sasha was always on time, whatever the vagaries of weather and public transport systems!

Finally, when Sasha's frail body let him down, he claimed the hospital as his new mission field, doing what he could for others. Even in death his witness was powerful. Joseph conducted the first Salvation Army funeral for more than 70 years, honoured to mark the promotion to Glory of this faithful young Salvationist.

Many young people were without parents. They had escaped from overcrowded community flats where they had come last in the pecking order, or fled stifling State orphanages where they had been dumped, for the freedom of the streets. Some survived with remarkable buoyancy. Others sank into a twilight world and were used and abused by streetwise mates and older, ruthless criminals.

Proposals for a shelter for such children were part of the expansion plan and Julia Wall came from England to put the plan into action. What a task for an attractive nurse from Harrow! Arriving in October 1993 she soon summed up the situation. The joy and positive spirit she found among her Christian friends at Sokolniki Corps contrasted sharply with the hopelessness she saw deep in the eyes of children she was trying to help.

The plight of these children moved Julia and her colleagues deeply. Plastic toys and packets of sweets did little to solve the problems of these elfin-faced waifs. Even the warm clothes they fitted them with were often sold by parents or older siblings for vodka-money before their next visit. Livid bruises indicated any claim to their right to keep them.

In other cases mothers or, more often, grandmothers relied on their children to beg or steal, instructing them in the pitiful speech and woeful look which moved sensitive travellers to give. Parents even resented Julia's team taking children away for a treat now and then, but in spite of this she arranged birthday trips to MacDonald's or picnics on a lawn near Paveletsky Station, much to the children's delight. Telling Bible stories to these largely uneducated children, who were hearing them for the first time, she found especially wonderful.

Prayer support was requested and given, and by April some rooms had been secured. Extensive repairs and decoration were carried out largely by volunteers. A doctor and four case-workers were employed and the centre was opened by Commissioner Schurink on 14 July 1993. The shelter was situated in a ground-floor apartment, simply furnished to house 10 children, with club facilities offering crafts, music, drama and games for others who lived in the neighbourhood. Weakened by neglect or aged by responsibility, the homeless youngsters were soon restored physically by good food, care and medical treatment. Damaged personalities were not so easily healed. Julia and her helpers were often at their wits end when dealing with the 'enraged, hurt and despairing' young people she described in a *War Cry* article.

Anxious to make a better future for at least a few of Moscow's destitute children, Julia worked to reunite with their families those who came to the shelter or, where this was not desirable, to find a new family who would accept them. Much as the vast majority of Russians value children and take their upbringing seriously, this was not an easy task. But one child was successfully placed in a children's home and six others were reunited with parents.

Within months the tolerance of neighbours had been worn down and eviction from the shelter followed. The sense of failure when the door closed weighed heavily. Not only those who had lived in the home but also the local children who enjoyed coming regularly to the day club would miss the support they had received.

Now Julia's parish was the street and the station, alongside Ivy and her assistant, Vasily. She gained a better understanding of the young people's lives, talking, eating, drinking and walking with them in their daily haunts. A favourite place was outside MacDonald's in Pushkin Square – a prime site for those who lived by their wits by relying on the generosity of others. One ploy was to jump the long queue and purchase burgers and fries for wealthy Muscovites waiting nearby in the warmth of their limousines. The tip they received for such service was well worth the wrath of McDonald's bouncers!

Julia's diary speaks volumes:

10 am: At the office there is paper-work to be done. Often there are newspaper and television reporters wanting interviews.

12 noon: After a prayer my assistant and I walk the streets, the stations and the Metro in search of children. At first contact we usually give them fruit, sweets or medical aid, which are a good ice-breaker.

We meet a nine-year-old boy begging alone for bread. His mother has been away from Moscow for two days searching for a place to live. The boy has not eaten since she left. He is not accustomed to street life and is quite frightened. We take him to a local cafe for a hot meal and he begins to talk to us more freely. We give him enough food for the day and arrange to meet him again in the evening.

4 pm: I dash home for my Russian lesson. This is much more exhausting than walking the streets! I have a quick bite to eat and then set off in search of children again.

7 pm: We try to do evening outreach twice a week. Tonight is good. After praying and asking God to lead us to the boy we met earlier, we find him and his mother, who has returned, together with two brothers and a sister. They are all dirty, tired and lice-ridden. The situation is desperate. She has found nowhere to live. The children are in need of warm coats and boots so we arrange to pick up some items from our clothing distribution centre the next day and take them to the family.

I feel so helpless at such times. Yet being close to the children and playing with them seems to bring them some comfort.

9 pm: I set off for home. If I've had no time to eat, I usually buy an ice-cream on the way. I know it sounds crazy, but Russians love ice-cream all year round and it's the most popular item sold on the street. Once home I relax a little and watch some television. I wear hearing aids and here there is an advantage in being deaf – when watching programmes originally made in English on Russian TV I can turn down the volume and lip-read!

Julia also recalls taking Andre, Kola and Alosha to the Army's clothing store. The delight on their faces when being fitted with 'new' clothes could not have been greater had they been taken into Harrods! Equally thrilled was a boy who was almost completely deaf. Communicating in a universal sign language, Julia managed to assess his need and provide hearing aids which made all the difference to his previously silent life.

The Médecins Sans Frontières group gave valued support to Salvationists working at the stations. One such incident occurred during the relentless heat of a Moscow summer. A baby's reaction as Julia touched him alerted her to blistered, raw skin beneath his T-shirt. Nursing experience told her that the situation was critical. The little boy needed medical care at once but the parking lot where the charity's mobile clinic usually stood was empty.

Briefly but forcefully, Julia prayed. She opened her eyes to see the vehicle drive past! By now the baby's mother had returned, showing surprise at all the fuss. Unknown to her the child had second-degree burns which could have killed him, had he not been treated.

So Julia's days passed. Persistent, caring application to need earned the trust not only of street people themselves but of militia, railway and health-care personnel. Team members were allowed to visit the militia's children's room at the stations to back up the inadequate care which overstretched staff had been able to give children abandoned or in trouble. The acquisition of a van, purchased with money raised in England, to replace Ivy's sturdy but small Lada made the work much easier. Containers of hot soup and trays of bread fitted into the back with supplies of clothing stowed behind them. Even before the Army van appeared at Paveletski or Kurski Stations a straggle of people would collect at the parking place, improvised plastic containers in hand. Hot soup and a hunk of bread would sustain them for a while.

Questions were asked as to the value of such a basic service. These people needed far more than soup, bread and sympathy. No one was more aware of this than those who looked into the dull eyes of those they served. How they longed for resources which were common to The Salvation Army in prosperous countries! As it was, they did what they could in the name of the One who knew the value of a cup of cold water.

On occasions the van became an ambulance. Arriving with a casualty at a hospital, one person talked persuasively to the receptionist while another stayed in the van, praying earnestly that the patient would be admitted! Amazing things happened. Experience taught Julia not to be surprised.

Now and then young men contacted by Julia's team would turn up at Sokolniki Corps. Gradually they grew in confidence and joined in meetings and Bible study. Delighted, Julia asked why they came. They replied that people were friendly and accepted them; they enjoyed learning about the Bible and asking questions; they liked singing – and all the pretty girls! Whatever their reasons, Julia knew that anything which brought them into a safe environment and gave them moments of happiness could be of lasting value.

A counselling session for homeless people was introduced, while discussion groups which guided young people on social issues, pointing out the Christian viewpoint on drug abuse and relationships, were regularly held.

Julia was a valued member of Sokolniki Corps. Using the language of movement, she taught young Christians whom Captain Pamela Smith had already recruited to communicate the gospel in dance, adding a new and effective dimension to worship in the corps and beyond.

Eventually Julia would be leaving to train as a Salvation Army officer in England. Amid the disappointment of goals unreached would be the knowledge that her Russian colleagues would continue to take light into dark places, kindling a spark of hope for the future.

Valuable prison work was carried out in Moscow, as in St Petersburg. The huge yet grosssly overcrowded Boutike Jail in Moscow was for most people a forgotten corner of the city. Once there was the possibility of co-operation with prison authorities, seminars were arranged by Captain Joseph Smith and other Army leaders to educate new Salvationists in methods of serving prisoners, helping them to see that in Christ there is hope for even the most degenerate.

A demoralised workforce was trying to contain a disintegrating penal system. The prison had been built in 1770 to house 3,000 prisoners in very basic conditions. Now up to 7,000 men were crowded into gloomy cells, some of which held 100 inmates who slept in shifts in the 30 or 40 bunks. One toilet and a washbasin completed the facilities. No one was allowed out for exercise. Food was an unrelieved diet of bread, soup or porridge and little medical treatment was available. Some prisoners were in their early teens. The only concession to their youth was to house them in small groups of six or eight.

In an attempt to raise morale among prison staff, who were paid a pittance, and to gain the confidence of the governor the Army supplied them with a share of the humanitarian-aid food. Permission was then given for entry into the jail.

The visitors discovered darkness – both literal and metaphorical. Every weekday a team visited the cells, bringing a ray of hope. Physically, the prisoners' lives were improved with gifts of soap, toothpaste, clothes and electric light bulbs. Medicines, donated by the Dutch Red Cross, were given to prison doctors. As a sign of trust, the Army was given warehouse facilities and an office in the prison compound.

There was a great need for spiritual support too. Christian literature was distributed and inmates were encouraged to study God's word. After gospel meetings held inside the jail the visitors reached out a hand of friendship. A part-time chaplain – Valentin Karuchin, a soldier of Moscow Central Corps – was appointed and evangelistic resources were supplied by other Christian groups and individuals who were concerned about those locked away from society. One individual gave more than 10,000 New Testaments in the first year. Another donated Bible study courses, taken up by 650 inmates.

The needs of the dependent families of prisoners, suffering harsh sentences themselves, were the next challenge. Women volunteers distributed food and clothing to them, offering support in times of crisis such as when a trial or review of sentence was to take place. A self-help group was set up so that families could encourage each other. As months passed many former prisoners found their way to Army centres to renew links which had meant so much to them.

The seed sown bore fruit in the lives of hundreds of remand prisoners who went to other prisons all over Russia to serve their sentences. Captain Smith, reflecting on his own conversion as a youthful prisoner wrote, 'Who would dare to set a limit on what God can do through prisoners who are now Christians in the Russian penal system!'

The volatile area of Central Asia became unstable in the late 1980s as the strong hand of Russian control loosened its grip. Ethnic strife coupled with the withdrawal of economic ties from the USSR brought an already poor area to desperate straits. The Salvation Army was among those sent to provide relief. Thus, when Commissioner Schurink travelled to Tblisi, Georgia, as part of his tireless quest to open doors for the gospel he received a welcome from President Edouard Shevardnadze.

Captain Mike Olsen directed 3,000 tons of food aid from the American government, through SAWSO (Salvation Army World Services Office), the Army's relief agency, to war-torn Georgia, in this case preceding spiritual ministry with social care. A chartered plane from Norway also brought clothes, baby food and soya protein. Everything was stored by the sackful in warehouses provided by the authorities and distributed as systematically as possible. It was a gigantic task to feed and clothe refugees from primitive mountain villages who were packed into concrete tower blocks in the city. Often electricity and water supplies were cut off, making life even more difficult for everyone.

Captain Ron Lee, his wife Linda and David, their teenage son, left the fledgling Pushkin Corps in St Petersburg and travelled south to Tblisi in July 1993 to develop the Army's work in Georgia and open a corps as soon as possible. When Commissioner Schurink made another flying visit he found the small airport at full stretch. Trucks marked with the Army red shield plied between airfield and city warehouse, loaded with humanitarian aid. On one journey, the 'cargo' was different. A wounded man was among 250 women and children who had flown, seated on the aircraft floor, from the area of conflict. The man was transferred to hospital far more quickly than had he waited for an ambulance to arrive. Another plane, full of soldiers, was waiting on the tarmac. Seizing an opportunity, the commissioner boarded the plane, by invitation, and spoke to the men of the Army of peace to which he belonged. His sincere prayer for God's guidance and protection was deeply appreciated by the men. The Christian church in Georgia is one of the oldest in the world, and the nation had not lost its sensitivity to God's Spirit.

The Tblisi Corps, which opened on 31 October, won and nurtured many fine Salvationists who understood what it means to be 'saved to serve'. When, a year later, Lieut-Colonel James Jay, who was then responsible for the command's finance and property matters, conducted with his wife, Lillian, the first anniversary a fine crowd of more than 100 stood and witnessed in the centre of the city. There was no doubt in Georgia of the purpose of this Army of peace.

In Ukraine, the Ljungholms moved to Kiev they soon planned a social programme to address some of the needs of that historic city. Before long, Captain Lois Dueck was appointed to develop the work. Coming as she did from the highly-organised and sophisticated Canada, Ukraine held many challenges for Lois but these spurred her on rather than deterred her.

By the end of September an office had been found and the Ukraine Social Service Department was installed. Valentine and Tatiana Zhurova and Vera Petrovich worked with Lois to set an effective programme in motion.

If anything, conditions of the poorest people of the community were even worse than those in Russia. Although Ukraine had rich resources, these had been drained when the country was part of the USSR and rebuilding them would be a long, hard process. Inflation was rampant and basic commodities like fuel oil, electricity and gas were severely rationed even for those who could afford them.

Lois knocked at government doors to seek support. It was important to help officials understand the vision of a better society which she wanted to work towards. Newspapers and TV programmes began to take up the theme as it became evident that The Salvation Army was making an impact in the city in many ways with family support, feeding programmes, home care for invalids, soup runs at the train station and prison visits. Ukrainians were eagerly learning at a series of seminars and then getting intensely involved.

Igor and Irena Skolotov were among those moved to do all they could to help. Irena was a trained teacher of the deaf and invited her pupils to attend Kiev I corps, signing the gospel message for them in the meetings. Her husband gained insight into the lives of homeless, displaced people as he helped distribute food in the streets.

In spite of repeated invitations, street people didn't attend meetings at the corps. They found it hard to integrate with those who were secure in home and family and also with a structured group, as the two Kiev corps now were. Suspicious of officials from unpleasant, even cruel, encounters, Lois's people needed their own group. It had taken months to build some element of trust. So she formed a corps just for them.

Meeting where they felt most at home – in the open air – they sang, accompanied by Lois on the accordion, prayed and listened to God's word. Some stayed on for Bible study, grouped by a wall, listening intently to new discoveries about God and his purpose for them. Knowing that a building would be needed for winter months, Lois and her staff searched fruitlessly for weeks. No property owner welcomed people like these.

When in 1994 Scottish Salvationist Andrew Eveleigh visited Kiev on an aid mission with a team from Edinburgh, Kiev's twin city, he worshipped with the street people's corps – named Mayak (Lighthouse) Corps – in the car park where they had been meeting for six months: 'Even on a late November afternoon, when the temperature was struggling to reach freezing point, about 100 homeless people stood in that car park for a half-hour service, after which they were given a bag of food. Then at least 75 of them stayed on for 45 minutes of Bible study,' he wrote, continuing, 'As it got darker and colder you could see the commitment shown by Captain Dueck and her workers.'

The following Sunday Andrew returned to rejoice with the corps on its first anniversary, celebrating too the fact that an indoor meeting-place had finally been secured.

Two years later Lieut-Colonel Bill Hunter, succeeding Colonel Hickam as General Secretary of the Command, visited Mayak Corps with his wife, Barbara. Moved to see Lois still working among the soldiers of this unconventional corps, Bill wrote about what he saw that day. His poem called 'A Chaos of Uniform' described the Ukrainian Salvationists in this poverty-stricken corner of the city. It concluded:

> This chaos of uniform
>> will never do for the cadets
>> will never be approved by the band board
>> might cause Trade to have a sale
>
> But today I saw the uniform
> As never before.
> Through tears I saw
>> the witness
>> the joy
>> the privilege . . .

During his visit Andrew Eveleigh was moved by other aspects of the Army's social work: ministry in a prison outside Kiev where 100 inmates attended Bible study and where they were helped to plant a beautiful garden; visits to hospitals which were supported with desperately-needed supplies when possible; a first-aid and bathing facility for rootless people, set up in co-operation with local services; help with the tedious and frustrating process of obtaining identity papers.

When Captains Mike and Ruth Olsen left Kiev for a new appointment in the States they looked back over a busy and productive period in the region. It ended with the enrolment of new senior and junior soldiers and the opening of Dneitzer Outpost at Left Bank Corps. UK officer Major Mrs Sheila Groom, whose last three years of service prior to retirement were spent in command, had been transferred from Babushkino Corps in Moscow to plant the outpost. Now she was handing over to Captain Liliane Pollock prior to taking on responsibility for the region's social services.

Faithful, appropriate service had gained increasing co-operation from the government at all levels, so much so that Lois's dream of a residential rehabilitation centre for men came slowly into being. A derelict property standing on agricultural land some way out of Kiev had become available. The dirty, leaking, unproductive property was a godsend to people with energy and vision. Together with a Ukrainian Salvationist whose life had been changed radically since discovering Christ, a small group of men camped at the property, cooking outdoors, while working hard to restore it before winter set in. Each time Lois visited the place, often taking others to witness the miracle, she saw another step in achievement. As the building was transformed, so those who worked gained confidence and self-respect. The house became the centre of a place of healing. Dry land, nurtured into the rich productivity for which Ukraine is known, supported men whose despair changed to hope.

Yalta, situated on the Black Sea, with a warm climate, was probably best known as a summer resort frequented by senior party members in Communist times. Now much of the past glory had gone. Hotels once the height of fashion were shabby, their gardens unkempt. Rusting ships languished in the harbour. It would take many years to burnish the jewel of the Black Sea coast again.

There were derelict humans in the town too, brought low by lack of work. When Majors Jake and Camie Bender arrived they soon realised there was plenty for them to do to fulfil the expectations of people who knew something of the Army's caring ministry through contact with 'General' Vladimir Mikhailovich and his friends. Gradually they taught that their primary aim was to lead people to spiritual growth and understanding. Through this teaching some Salvationists realised that they could help their neighbours in practical ways themselves, not relying entirely on gifts from abroad.

Victoria was a new Salvationist. Frequently she passed a wrecked shed near rubbish bins which was home to two men.

They were the kind of men she would have avoided before becoming a Christian. They were sick, filthy and hungry. To eat they had to compete with stray cats for garbage. Compassion aroused, each day Victoria took porridge, soup and tea for the men but she felt she could do more with help from the officers. They went along with her to meet the men and, seeing their great need, gave Victoria food and clothing for them. As she came to know them she tried a bit of the discipline she used on her young orphaned twin granddaughters, insisting that they cleaned up after themselves, washed their dishes and took a weekly bath at the public baths.

The men's self-respect slowly returned as Victoria put into practice a Salvation Army motto: 'With heart to God and hand to man.'

Five hundred miles south of Moscow in Volgograd, the Army was given the use of a brightly-painted, well-kept building, a former kindergarten in a busy area. There were great possibilities for developing a community service programme. A fault in the hot-water system which persisted for months caused delays but once this was solved the work grew.

Captains Tom and Laura Lyle, with Jerry and Anna Redmond, who had moved from Ekaterinburg, laid foundations on which Captains Chuck and Candi Smalley were able to build. Good, hot meals were regularly supplied to elderly people who were able to stay and enjoy good company, adding to the usual food and clothing distributions which met a great need in the district. Especially valued was a group for physically disabled children who enjoyed therapy and education given by trained staff. Their families appreciated the sense of worth and acceptance they felt at the Army which contrasted with the isolation their children's disabilities had previously caused.

The same caring spirit was developed in every corps and outpost. Carefully assessing needs, pioneering officers recruited and trained willing workers, both Salvationists and other

Christians, and used resources in the best way they could. God's continual supply of strength and resources gave them the ability to fulfil Christ's words: 'Inasmuch as ye have done it unto one of the least of these my brethren, ye have done it unto me' (Matthew 25:40, *AV*).

Chapter 12

ROOTS

Young Christians nurtured in faith

GENYA and his four brothers and sisters lived a full life. Their parents, Boris and Sasha, worked hard to keep the family in harmony. In post-Communist Moscow money had to be stretched much further than in the early years of their marriage, but they had a good apartment in a northern suburb of the city and there were many positive things happening.

As Sasha watched her younger children cross the yard to the nearby school, colourful rucksacks on their backs, she wondered what direction they would take in life. She and her husband had entered fully into a wealth of educational, cultural and leisure activities when they were that age. Lenin, like others with a sociological vision, knew the importance of influencing children. Like the majority, Sasha trusted her leaders and believed in her country but also she had seen the cracks and imperfections.

Now the old edifice had crumbled and there was opportunity to create a new society. Guiding their own children through the trauma of adolescence, Boris and Sasha understood that the nation's transition would be difficult too. God, whose sovereignty had been scorned, must be enthroned again. Eternal values – truth, compassion, honesty – were those which mattered. Sasha looked for people who would teach these qualities by word and action.

129

Then they heard about The Salvation Army. Careful investigation showed that this was one of many Christian groups crowding into Russia but, unlike some, it had a long track record and a reputation for adding good works to faith. Visiting Moscow Central Corps, which had just opened in the city, they were attracted by the joyful style of worship, and the hubbub of purposeful activity. Kathy Ljungholm soon recruited Genya (the model of an angelic choirboy!) for the singing company. His parents judged that in this company their family would be led in the right direction following in the footsteps of Jesus.

In many corps of the command children were among the first to become involved. Some came because a link was formed when families received food and clothing from Salvation Army warehouses. (Lest anyone accuse the Army of creating 'rice-Christians' – those who become followers simply to obtain material benefits – they must realise that had this been so, many thousands would have flocked to meetings! Congregations were probably smaller in the areas where the most food was distributed.) Other children were invited by friends or were attracted by open-air meetings. The English language was another attraction. It was seen as the key to many opportunities for both work and leisure. Just to hear it spoken by those for whom it was the first language was fascinating to those who, until then, had heard it spoken only by Russian linguists. Parents seeing this as a good educational extra did not always become aware of the truth Salvationists wanted to convey, but some absorbed the message as well as the language.

In St Petersburg, the first Sunday school grew rapidly. Attractive, effective teaching methods were soon absorbed by young Russians who then took over the responsibility for teaching groups of children, divided according to age. A singing group was formed and there was a great demand for timbrels to enable more children to learn the skill which they were proud to demonstrate in open-air meetings as well as indoors.

All these activities were founded on a comprehensive teaching programme of Bible study, Christian living and Salvation Army practice devised by the Ryans and Minna Karlström, largely from Canadian sources.

Primorsky, St Petersburg South and Pushkin Corps each developed a children's programme, some based on weekday club activities, others on a more traditional Sunday school, according to the type of community and premises available. Many children, backed by believing parents, signed the junior soldier promise acknowledging Jesus as their friend and saviour. Continuing interest, Christian education and example helped them develop into fine, active members of corps and community.

Pioneering officers and their staff went to great lengths to organise special events for children and young people. Phil Wall and Mission Team members from the United Kingdom Territory were warmly welcomed to St Petersburg a number of times. Their lively style of evangelism drew an enthusiastic response from those who were throwing off the formal style of education and entertainment which had been normal in Communist times.

By spring 1994 there were expressions of Salvation Army ministry in places far from the bustling cities where it was easier for Salvationists to meet together. It would be marvellous if young people who worshipped and worked in comparative isolation could come together for a weekend. It was a great idea, but what about visas, transport, accommodation, language, leadership? The whole scheme could have remained just a good idea but, holding on to the reminder that with God all things are possible, the proposal was accepted and put into practice.

Majors Keith and Beryl Burridge from the UK's South London Division accepted the invitation to lead youth councils and brought not only themselves but books, a binding machine for the resource centre and other evidences of goodwill from their division.

Right on schedule young people from Kiev, Tblisi, Volgograd, Voronesh, Ekaterinburg, St Petersburg and Moscow arrived at a splendid conference centre at Aksakova in the countryside north of Moscow. There was no doubt of God's presence either. The natural reticence of this disparate group soon melted when delegates discovered that they knew the same songs, albeit in different languages, and were seeking the same goals.

The countryside declared that summer had arrived, although a cold wind still claimed that winter had not quite retreated. Recognising that the Church had recently celebrated Easter, it was suggested that footpaths around Aksakova become the road to Emmaus. With groups of new friends, young people walked the paths, stopping here and there as cadets, using inspiration and imagination, introduced them to events and characters from the account of that first Easter and then asked the delegates to make the experience personal. How would they have reacted? Would they have recognised Jesus in those circumstances? Did they recognise him now? In quietness, Jesus drew near to many young people that day as they stood by the wind-ruffled lake or among shimmering birch trees.

His presence was felt as people conversed at the meal table, gathered for unscheduled prayer, studied the Bible and responded to the clear challenge to walk the Christian way. For some, this meant officership, and many names were added to the list of prospective candidates that weekend.

All too quickly the event was over and delegates made their way home. They had left behind prayers, placed on a large 'prayer tree'. As these were translated in the youth office, a prayer of thanks was breathed. With God, amazing things were possible!

Encouraged by the success of early Army camps in St Petersburg, other regions planned their own. By the summer of 1994 Moscow Corps had enrolled dozens of junior soldiers, most of whom went eagerly to camp at a country site in July. The facilities, a former Pioneer camp which had been spared the decay into which some of these fine complexes had fallen, were impressive. The indoor swimming pool, large meeting hall, dining room which supplied hearty meals, roomy dormitories and attractive grounds came alive that week!

A happy mix of active learning, sport and relaxation kept children and adults occupied. Newly-commissioned lieutenants slipped easily into leadership. They had experienced the fun of organised outdoor life as young Pioneers. Now their motivation was a personally-chosen faith. They were glad to be entrusted with showing the new way to another generation.

Co-operating with the Russians was an American Service Corps team whose members worked and played, taught and learnt in a whirl of purposeful activity. A ramble with a picnic, campfires, talent competitions, fancy dress, and a 'do-it-yourself' pageant, craft and music on a Salvation Army theme, contrasted with quiet, serious moments of worship and Bible study to complete a memorable week.

As the junior soldiers left, more children arrived for a camp arranged by Captains Joseph and Pamela Smith and the social services department. Many of them had a parent in prison and desperately needed the carefree atmosphere of days in country air, good food and sensitive teaching about the God who cares for them in every circumstance.

Some camps majored in music, giving excellent opportunity for concentrated singing, playing and drama which numerous children from Russia and other CIS countries enjoy. The music camp in Kiev, supported by Winton Salvationists, was just one such example, while the team responsible for South London Division's school of music were invited to staff a camp in Moscow. They knew that in many ways the experience would be a contrast to their British event but they discovered that the interest and concentration of Russian young people was equally inspiring.

Finding it impossible to rent a suitable residence, Janet Gilson and her team, with great co-operation from corps officers, soldiers and staff at the Lublino school, ran the music camp in the school premises, the children returning to their homes each evening.

From the first day the spirit of unity between East and West was obvious. As the week progressed, more children found their way to the school and in the final festival a great chorus matched the *Sister Act* choir of Whoopi Goldberg's movie, surprising the congregation with their skill and verve. 'For God so loved the world' they sang. The faces of eager eight-year-olds and thoughtful teenagers reflected their own response to the wonder of these words.

'See you next year!' The words were heard again and again as the team, comprising of Captains Rik and Chris Pears, Mike and Stuart Kirk from Peterborough, Mark Walton, Hazel Ball, Joan Spencer and Nik Pears, all from South London corps, said farewell.

How could they stay away? After a year of fund-raising and personal saving most of them were back for the following year's camp. This was housed in a Moscow music institute in very basic accommodation such as only students would identify with! During the day every available corner echoed with music. On the stairs a trombone section practice would be in progress. In a lobby guitars were strummed while fingers were coaxed into the correct positions on the strings. Timbrels, dance, song, recorders, percussion, keyboard all competed for space in the dusty old building. Daily Bible studies titled 'The race is on' reflected the fact that it was 1996, an Olympic summer.

At the final festival in Moscow the whole week's music-making and study were woven together in harmony. Each delegate was urged to carry the light of God's love into the world to draw people together as the Olympic torch had done in Atlanta.

The Olympic state of Georgia, USA, felt an affinity with Georgia, CIS, and many exchange visits between the two were made. The Army was involved in this plan. Captains Alex and Luz Nesterenko, South American officers who had joined the pioneering forces in Tblisi in October 1993, arranged a series of conferences and camps high in the mountains. While a seminar for local officers took place, American young people kept the

134

delegates' children busy with a programme of Christian teaching and sport. Each evening other children and young people, resident at the sanatorium where the camp was held, joined in a session of lively worship which threatened to raise the roof!

Having seen the style of the Service Corps teams, Russian young people decided this was the kind of ministry they could be involved in themselves. There would be an ideal opportunity when the Goodwill Games were held in St Petersburg in the summer of 1994.

Susan Harris, a young Salvationist from Coventry, England, whose close involvement with teenagers at Moscow Central had taught her so much, nervously took on the responsibility of leading a team. Meeting regularly, they developed a series of mimes with a message and other tactics for arresting the attention of passing crowds. Terri Lines, an Australian youth leader working in St Petersburg Region, welcomed Susan and her team and set them to work with a busy schedule. The mission was used by God to interest and inspire people from the far reaches of the CIS in the gospel. It was a thrilling but exhausting experience which added to the preparation which some of the team members were making to become Salvation Army officers.

Later, a team of Georgian Salvationists with a number from other parts of the command, had an exciting week supporting the Army's ministry at the Olympic Games in Atlanta, USA. Instead of distributing hot soup, which was the norm in their experience, they dispensed gallons and gallons of cold water to thirsty spectators. It was another example of the internationalism of this movement whose red shield logo is recognised by people from at least a hundred nations.

Other candidates and a number of lieutenants travelled even further on a mission to encourage fellow Salvationists. Commissioner Schurink, now in retirement and running a corps back in his home territory, The Netherlands, longed for Dutch people to have first-hand experience of the miracle he witnessed in Russia and the

CIS. The candidates secretary, Major Janet Gilson, in consultation with their corps officers, selected a group of young people from among many fine Salvationists throughout the command. Captain Wendy Walters, soon to succeed her in that position, completed the group. It was a memorable excursion for everyone concerned. Hospitality at a number of Dutch Salvation Army centres opened new horizons on methods of Christian ministry. The exemplary deportment of the Russian, Ukrainian, Georgian and Moldovan Salvationists and their moving testimonies inspired the Dutch as Commissioner Schurink had expected. As they stood, faces lit by the glow of candles, singing of the Holy Spirit, he prayed that the flame of faith would continue to burn, destroying sin and ignorance wherever the young people went.

The busy youth and children's programme, set up and implemented by Major Gilson for three years and continued by Captain Rodney Walters (in addition to other responsibilities at command headquarters) after his term in St Petersburg, was backed up by resources and training wherever possible. Experienced reinforcement officers came with a store of ideas, books and visual aids and staff undertook the time-consuming job of translation. Even the best materials were not always appropriate. Although rapidly changing, Eastern bloc countries were used to a vastly different style of education and leisure. Made aware of the need, USA Eastern Territory funded a resource centre as part of command headquarters. Using a new computer with desktop publishing software Masha Shostak, a 16-year-old soldier of Moscow Central Corps, taught herself step by step to produce illustrated Bible teaching materials and activity leaflets for children to take home, reinforcing the lessons. These were based on Scripture Union resources, already used in a number of Army territories, and adapted for use in this specific situation. Katia Ivanova worked tirelessly, when her university timetable allowed, translating page after page. A chance encounter Masha had on a metro train brought Boris Skvortsov, another language student, to the office to help.

Scripture Union representatives, looking for ways of providing Russian language teaching material, appreciated what was being developed and made a contract to help with translation costs in return for a supply of the finished notes and leaflets for distribution in other churches. This was an encouraging arrangement. It meant that some progressive Orthodox Christians, open to new ideas, were among those happy to receive help with their teaching programme.

Basic junior soldier and corps cadet resources were made available, as well as suggestions for children's club and camp activities to spark off ideas. Russian was not the only language to be used in the command. Where possible, arrangements were made to assist with funding for translation in the early days. Georgians were pleased when certificates, songs, Bible lessons and an evangelical newspaper appeared in their own language, translated largely by Tsisi, a Salvationist who had been employed at regional headquarters by Captain Lee. Ukrainians and Moldovans also preferred to use their own languages now that Russian was no longer compulsory.

Gradually the range of Protestant Christian publications in each language increased to meet the great demand. Many had been published abroad, although bringing books through customs caused problems. Now a number of publishers and distributors within the CIS were becoming more productive. The 'Bibles for All' shop in St Petersburg, tucked away in an insignificant corner of the city, contained some rare treasures of Scripture teaching. A basement store run by the Protestant Publishing House in Moscow was also stocked with books, posters, videos and music tapes for those who sought information and inspiration.

The Russian Bible Society had been revived after more than a hundred years and was purposefully engaged in preparing new translations of the Bible in classic modern Russian in a lasting binding. It was good to handle such quality publications. The first Bibles to be widely available in the USSR after perestroika were hastily-prepared paperback editions sent in from abroad. These were highly valued at the time, but the scholarship and craftsmanship in the Bible Society publications were of lasting worth. All of these items were promoted by the Army's Resource Centre.

In one corner of the office Svetlana Ivanova prepared *Vestnik Spasseniya* for publication, including in its pages encouraging news from all parts of the command. Misha Gavrilov, sergeant-major of Moscow Central Corps and a graphic artist by profession, had also joined the staff. His joy in discovering God through his word reflected in Misha's artwork. A particular Bible verse would catch his imagination and after a period of gestation Misha would work in the small studio corner of the apartment he shared with his wife, Valentina, and translate the words into colour and form.

One by one the office walls were adorned with Misha's posters, silent messages to all who paused to look at them. They spoke to General Paul Rader when he entered the office on his first visit to command headquarters, with the consequence that Misha carried out more than one commission for the General's office. Whether designing the coloured publicity brochure for distribution throughout the command or a poster to be used once, Misha worked meticulously. Since his conversion his work for a new Master had given him great fulfilment. When Valentina joined him, some months later, as a soldier of Moscow Central Corps he was very proud. Her Christian influence as director of a large kindergarten was recognised and respected.

Until new legislation curtailed publishing activities of selected groups, including The Salvation Army, the resource team busily worked to prepare material to back up the teaching ministry of the command. Candidate Edic Kusnetsov prepared a brass instrument learning course and young Genya experimented with video during school holidays, with the minimum of technology filming and editing sensitive records of Salvationists in action.

It was essential that new Salvationists were personally guided and trained to teach children rather than just using material from the centre and be left to work things out for themselves. Teachers were needed at once, so in the early days there had been no long course or period of observation. As soon as they claimed conversion, those with aptitude were made responsible for a group of children and attended lesson preparation week by week in an officer's apartment or a corner of a rented building. Usually they were just one or two steps in front of the children and learnt as much as they taught!

As the structure of the command came into place, more formal training was offered as often as possible. Sometimes corps officers prepared and led their own courses. Others invited regional or command staff to help. Captain Janette Shepherd, an Australian officer, was responsible for co-ordinating training events in various parts of the command. She co-opted staff from the college when there was no session of cadets in progress, as well as Command leaders Colonels Brian and Carolyn Morgan and other CHQ staff members. Courses helped Salvationists to deepen their understanding of the Christian faith, to explore different ways of expressing worship and methods of running the wide variety of programmes which could be introduced into an Army corps – home league, league of mercy, Bible study, music groups.

People eagerly gathered to learn how to teach. Ukrainians met in the splendid military officers centre in Kiev, Georgians gave a week of holiday time at a sanatorium with very basic facilities and Salvationists at Yalta, including 'General' Vladimir Mikhailovich, met in a room above a cafe overlooking the Black Sea, all with the same purpose – to learn the best way of presenting Christian teaching to children. These, and large numbers of others who took training opportunities, knew that children who, in many cases, had led the way into the brave new world of faith were precious. Only the best care would do for them as they grew into maturity as members of The Salvation Army.

One person who learnt more about the Christian faith as she taught children was Nellie, of Yalta Corps. Major and Mrs Bender knew that music appeals to children and hired Nellie, a professional teacher, to develop a singing group. She loved the children, visiting them when they were sick, and teaching them to pray as well as to sing. As their repertoire increased, the Benders and Nellie taught new songs to the adult congregation and visited hospitals and churches with the gospel message. All this time Nellie and her husband, encouraged and taught by the Benders whom they admired for their commitment to the Ukrainian people, were discovering what it means to be Salvationists. They claimed a new beginning the day they were enrolled as soldiers of Yalta Corps, setting a fine example for the children in their care to follow.

Many talented instrumentalists were given opportunities to develop their skills to use in God's service. The St Petersburg Central Band set the pace and that of Moscow's Presnia Corps followed, boosted by Australian experts, Captain Janette Shepherd, and Dion Boyd, a member of the Finance Department at headquarters, and Dion's head of department, Major Rob Garrad. Even Colonel Morgan 'had a blow' at Lublino when he was not elsewhere in the command. Anyone working late at CHQ on certain evenings was serenaded by a composite band trained by Edic Kusnetsov and Dion. It was clear that banding was in the blood of these musicians.

The rate of growth in the command was exceptional. Most of the corps enrolled more soldiers in one year than the majority of other European corps in 10. Leaders in the command and observers from other parts of the Army world knew that sound teaching and training were vital in order to ground both junior and senior soldiers firmly in the faith. Given this, the future of The Salvation Army in Russia/CIS would be secure.

Chapter 13

ASK . . . SEEK . . . KNOCK

New doors open in spite of hindrances

IN the dark month of February 1993 while cadets of the Heralds of Jesus Session were being trained, there came reminders that the presence of The Salvation Army in Russia and the CIS still could not be taken for granted. People and organisations felt threatened by the many foreign influences sweeping their country.

At a conference for religious groups held in Moscow this fear was expressed: 'Western missionaries and sectarians are inundating Russia,' claimed a spokesman of the Orthodox church. In one city Commissioner Schurink, seeking permission for the Army to open work, was shown a list of 54 Western churches applying for registration. No wonder there was concern! President Yeltsin, teetering towards an attempt to impeach him, needed to maintain good relationships with Orthodox church leaders but he did not want to discriminate against other religions and Christian denominations. This would be contrary to the spirit of glasnost.

In a nation which had had suppression enforced on it for so long, many attractive cults appeared on the scene once freedom was given. Astrology, mysticism and obscure Eastern cults all gained followers. To those leaders of the official church who made superficial enquiries about it, The Salvation Army with its flagrant proselytising and the powerful draw of quantities of humanitarian aid was as undesirable as the rest. At this stage the co-operation from foreign ministry officials was largely withdrawn making administration, including the processing of visas, more difficult. The office space which had been granted was now cut back.

In spite of these difficulties the Army continued to advance and people's lives were transformed. Captain Ljungholm, posted as Regional Commander for Ukraine and Moldova, and his wife had made their mark in Kiev. Ukraine was free from the shackles of Moscow's rule but its independence was at great economic cost. People who were quickly recruited to help with relief work caught the Army spirit and became soldiers. Kiev I Corps soon branched out across the Dneiper River and planted Kiev II Corps.

Lieutenants Philip and Svetlana Rybakov were commissioned to assist the Ljungholms. While adjusting to a new country, new baby Timothy, and a new vocation they still made a significant contribution to the development of the Army in Kiev, especially among children and young people. Once a week Kiev I took over a main street cafe for a youth outreach programme. The evening began with a corps cadet training session in Bible study and evangelism. Then teen music began, doors were opened and training was put into practice. Games, coke and crisps, quizzes and chat provided an attractive atmosphere for young Salvationists to make friends with newcomers and influence them for good. Kiev was a tough but effective learning experience. Philip and his wife realised its value when they later returned to Moscow to lead Babushkino Corps in the north of the city, which had been pioneered by Lieut-Colonels James and Lillian Jay and Major Mrs Sheila Groom.

Presnia Corps, originally called '1905' after the district in which it is situated, was now well-established, with some fine Russian local officers assisting Captains Mike and Ruth Olsen. Captain Glenda Daddow took over the leadership and Lieutenants Sasha and Maria Kharkov were appointed to work with her. Each Sunday the former Communist culture palace, almost under the shadow of the White House parliament building, came alive with Christian music, prayer and testimony. Professional people and stateless wanderers, young and old, all discovered Jesus there as Sasha and Maria cared for them.

The weekend, later that year, when the world woke to news that the White House was under siege, was particularly memorable for the people of Presnia Corps. The building they used was taken over by one of the factions in the dispute and Sasha had to make hurried arrangements for an alternative venue for worship. It was a tense episode, but the attempted political coup failed and with much relief the corps resumed its programme.

Lieutenant Yuri Chutkin was appointed as assistant to Captains Joseph and Pamela Smith who had established a new corps at Sokolniki. His knowledge would be invaluable to the captain as he searched for ways of improving social conditions for destitute, hopeless people in Moscow. Major Ivy Nash, with a long record of inner-city ministry in Britain, had also come to work with the captain in this area. Even to her experienced view the situation in Russia seemed almost hopeless. She and many of her friends back home prayed and believed for miracles – the posting of Julia Wall to Moscow had been one of the answers to her prayers.

Captains John and Narelle Rees from Australia took over responsibility for Moscow Central Corps in addition to co-ordinating Army work of all kinds in the city. New Zealander Major David Major, with his wife Carol, succeeded Major Gwynneth Evans as city co-ordinator for St Petersburg. Gwynneth could now give her full attention to developing Primorsky Corps with her assistant, British Salvationist Joy Farley.

The foundation corps in St Petersburg received newly-commissioned Lieutenant Yuri Sidorin in the summer to add to the leadership team Geoff and Sandra Ryan had built. Expatriate lay workers Helen Lucas from Australia and Adrian Allott from New Zealand were learning and working together with Russian Salvationists, maintaining a busy programme of worship, music evangelism, teaching, youth training, community service, publishing, and prison and hospital ministry.

Plans to move into the suburbs continued with the opening of Pushkin Corps by Captains Ron and Linda Lee, from the USA, assisted by Lieutenants Vladimir and Valerie Tateosov, who assumed charge when the Lees transferred to Georgia. Thirteen soldiers from St Petersburg Central, many of whom lived nearer to Pushkin, transferred to form a nucleus around which the new corps grew. Finnish graduate Minna Karlström returned to help as well.

St Petersburg South Corps was pioneered by Captain Denise McGarvey, a British officer. Grappling with the usual problems of bureaucracy and misunderstanding, each corps gradually built a viable ministry, supported by the regional headquarters team.

The visit of the St Petersburg Band and Timbrel Group to England, climaxing with their appearance at the farewell meeting of General Eva Burrows, indicated the fine quality and enthusiasm of Russian Salvationists.

Deputy Bandmaster Sergei Zhuravlyov was typical of young people who had grown up with little understanding of religion, absorbing the party line that only weak or strange people believed in God. He was born in Siberia, with a working-class background. His musical talent, which set him apart from most of his friends, was noticed and encouraged. Eventually he went to St Petersburg to continue studies in composition and trombone at the musical institute.

During a vacation in Siberia he attended a Pentecostal church. Although he had been baptised as a child in the Orthodox church this was the first time he had taken Christianity seriously. He was keen to learn more.

Back in St Petersburg, his friend Yuri invited him to The Salvation Army. At that point the main attraction was the music but gradually, as his sense of God's presence increased, he was aware of his own weakness. He repented of his sin and, step by step, took the path to soldiership.

When the visit to England was proposed Sergei set to work to compose a march especially for the campaign. This was no easy task but he finished the composition in time. In many venues excited applause greeted the band of eleven players as they sounded out the march, 'Return to Russia'.

A memorable tour of the UK by Moscow Central Singing Company under its leader, Olga Asanansieva, followed in July. In preparation, the children had made a recording in a Moscow studio which bore an uncanny resemblance to an English parish church, with a high beamed roof and neo-Gothic window arches. In fact, that is exactly what it was and a few months later Her Majesty Queen Elizabeth II accepted it back from city authorities on behalf of the Anglican parish of Moscow.

The singing company's tour began with a star appearance at the London welcome to General and Mrs Bramwell Tillsley and continued with whirlwind visits to seven British towns. Thousands who heard the young Muscovites singing gospel songs in both Russian and English were profoundly moved by the experience. It epitomised for them 'new Russia' where people were free to teach their children about Jesus.

An even deeper impression was made on those who welcomed singing company members into their homes. The young people's unsophisticated enjoyment of every new experience was infectious. Many links of friendship forged that week remain strong to this day. The children were proud to be Russian; in some ways their journey confirmed their identity but it demonstrated too the universal bond of Christian faith.

The sight and sound of those 60 young Russians remains vivid in the memory. Many still ask, 'What about the singing company?' For a number of reasons, the group which broke for the summer months after the tour didn't re-form in the autumn. Many were involved in crucial school and college study and others moved away but a nucleus remained, continuing to make music and serve God in several of the Moscow corps. The music tape they made in the old Anglican church still lifts the spirits of those who play it and generous financial support continues to come from many corps involved in hosting the tour.

These were just the first of many musical ambassadors to travel from Russia, Ukraine and other parts of the CIS. The spirit of Salvation Army friendship has been enriched by the warmth of their personalities while people have been drawn nearer to God through their music.

In Russia spring comes suddenly. In cities desert-like yards sprout fresh green overnight. Stark black branches sport a new pink, white and lime garment after a few days of warm southerly breezes. The countryside swarms with people digging and planting, weeding and watering, working for the harvest which sustains them during winter months.

Spring and summer 1993 brought rapid growth in the Army too. More personnel from overseas entered open doors in other parts of the CIS: Majors David and Carol Major in Minsk, with Australian Captains Rodney and Wendy Walters taking their place in St Petersburg; American Captains Tom and Laura Lyle journeyed south to Volgograd. Major Cindy Shellenberger pioneered in Ekaterinberg, (followed by experienced and practical Salvationists Jerry and Anna Redmond who later moved on to Volgograd), Majors Wesley and Ruth Sundin and Captain Lois Dueck were appointed to Kiev, and Majors Jake and Camie Bender to Yalta on the Crimean coast. South American officers, Captains Alex and Luz Nesterenko followed Captains Ron and Linda Lee to Tblisi, Georgia; Australian Captain Glenda Daddow was appointed to Moscow, and later, Ekaterinburg, and Canadian Major Sandra Foster went to Moscow to develop a senior citizens' programme.

Visas, luggage, transport, accommodation, programme support, finance – all this had to be provided for every person on the list. Command headquarters staff, in the small basement office not far from the Dynamo football stadium, worked at full stretch to enable it all to happen. Commissioner Schurink pursued each possibility with enthusiastic energy, travelling the land and finding the key to open many new doors. The Russia/CIS Command was undoubtedly on the map!

The miracle of the planting, growth and nurture of each new Army centre is a story in itself. The main goal of presenting people with the gospel in word and action and winning them for Christ was achieved in a variety of ways. Initial approaches were crucial. Once the euphoria of freedom had passed, people were cautious. They wanted genuine ideas, devoted leaders. Fine Russians, Ukrainians and Georgians found these in The Salvation Army and in turn committed themselves to leadership, many applying for officer-training. Salvationists worldwide continued to marvel at the way God was working in the former Communist bloc. Their prayers and financial support were invaluable.

For months negotiations had been taking place to purchase a building in Moscow for a permanent headquarters. Until the Communist structure collapsed, every building was State-owned. Now a complex move towards private ownership was in progress. The process was full of legal and financial pitfalls.

By the turn of the year, the contract was signed. As the lease of the basement office had run out, this was none too soon. Staff were already working from home, communicating by phone and sharing business meals in each other's quarters. There was great elation as they entered the door of Krestiansky Tupik 16/1 on 4 January 1994. The three-storey, four-square building which had been part of the estate of a nearby monastery in pre-revolution times gave a feeling of permanence and cohesion to the Army's work.

The doorkeeper was kept busy drawing the latch for a succession of people from early morning to late evening. A new session of cadets with their training principal, Australian Lieut-Colonel Lucille Turfrey, the Vanovers, Esther Washburn and newcomer Captain Sandra Reid from Canada, soon settled in the top-floor offices and classroom next to the youth and candidates secretary's busy office. The embryo resource centre was also sited there, where Svetlana Ivanova would produce *Vestnik Spasseniya* once again, alongside the director, Miriam Blackwell from England, who had the responsibility of reinforcing the teaching, evangelistic and music resources already available in the command. The finance department was on the ground floor with the *stolovar* and kitchen conveniently close while on the intermediate floor the officer commanding and general secretary worked with their supporting staff.

Armed guards, stamping in the cold outside the nearby militia depot looked out suspiciously from below grey fur hats. Who were these people in dark uniforms? There were a number of private security forces emerging in the city. Was this one of them? When a banner declaring *Armiya Spasseniya* in foot-high letters was hoisted outside the active, multi-national centre the mystery was solved. Those in the know told others that this Army was a Christian movement returning to the city to continue good work it had begun more than 70 years before. A few visits inside the building to use photocopying facilities confirmed their view that, as the law stood, they did not need to interfere with their new neighbours.

Others were not so neutral. A spate of vehicle thefts and burglaries of Army premises in a number of places caused dismay and inconvenience as well as much expense. Western vehicles and computer equipment were a sign of affluence. Thieves did not stop to think of the negative consequences their actions would have for vulnerable members of their own community.

The new building proved to be an oasis of calm. Even at times of intense activity, conflict and disappointment, God's presence was sensed within the sturdy walls, confirmed by prayer and praise.

Russian Salvationists were keen to develop skills and to offer them in service. Svetlana Ivanova had the joy of attending an

International Literary and Publications Conference in Washington in the spring of 1994. She was in her element – an intellectual among intellectuals of the Army world. The title of the conference, Writing the Vision, appealed to her as well. Giving her prepared testimony she spoke of running away into writing to escape an unhappy childhood. Later she could not escape from the vision of destitute people whom she had largely ignored by inhabiting her dream-world of fiction: 'The intellectual, economic and social atmosphere around me was in chaos. I was in crisis. I stopped reading, writing, meeting my friends. I even stopped sleeping. Nothing pleased me. It could have degenerated into tragedy if I had not met The Salvation Army,' she said, adding dramatically, 'Never will I forget that day. It was the hand of God showing me the way to escape.'

During Svetlana's term as editor and her soldiership of Moscow Central Corps she showed a deep and practical concern for disadvantaged people, keenly linking them to the Army's support system. Later the world of literature claimed her attention again, but her awareness of God, and knowledge of his Son, which she had gained from Bible study and worship, remained rooted deeply in her soul.

Another of those who found fulfilment as a Salvationist and made an important contribution to the Army's development in Moscow and beyond was Dina Bandukova. Smart and efficient, she was attracted by the first meetings in Moscow Central Corps. Her Orthodox background, which for years had been deeply hidden as she openly toed the party line, found an echo in the reverent prayer and joyful music of the Salvationists.

With characteristic enthusiasm she immersed herself in the Army programme and was soon spotted by Sven and Kathy Ljungholm. She would make an ideal trade secretary! The growing force needed to be equipped with uniforms, flags and badges. Would she take on the responsibility? Dina was happy to have been trusted with such an important task.

The first soldiers to be enrolled in St Petersburg were supplied with uniforms from Canada. Others were fitted with second-hand outfits which came in consignments from the West. With expansion of the Army's work it was important to have a steady supply from Russia itself. The Russian military force was being rapidly reduced – military tailors would be glad of some bespoke orders to keep them in business.

Dina set about her search, assisted by Olga Romantsova. Eventually five different factories were contracted to supply the necessary items: men's caps from one, soldiers' and officers' uniform suits from another, a third made hats for women and children, a fourth metal crests and badges, and a fifth embroidered insignia. The Trade Department of the UK Territory gave a bale of good 'Army serge'. Store rooms were rented and Dina was in business! Not only did she supply uniforms, she also appeared at each corps in Moscow when an enrolment was due to take place to ensure that they were correctly worn with dignity and grace!

Perhaps her greatest challenge, and a test of faith, related to her first assignment in October 1992. Orders for 100 new uniforms had been placed with a tailoring workshop in good time for the planned enrolment of soldiers. Then a serious accident occurred, killing two women workers. For safety reasons the workshop was closed and production of the uniforms stopped. This was a dilemma for Dina. With inflation running at 15-20 per cent per month it would be too costly to break the contract and approach a new firm with a plea for an express service. On the other hand, in this keen new Army it was unthinkable to be sworn in without uniform. Dina prayed earnestly and God heard and answered her prayers. She had obtained a bale of serge, and the factory reopened to make the uniforms only. The enrolment of 100 smartly-clad soldiers took place as planned.

In following years Dina found great satisfaction in this practical service. She would bustle into headquarters with a new style of jumper for winter wear, or a good line in black shoes she had discovered. Fitting out cadets gave her especial joy. Had she been younger she might well have trained as an officer herself. However her work, mundane as it might seem to one who had known privilege, was also for the Kingdom.

As each corps developed, people like Dina seemed to be marked out by God to take key roles. Officers were teamed with music leaders and Bible teachers, able administrators and trusted financiers, handymen and nurses to form the body of Christ, their diversity united in him. Where there was mutual respect which grew into love, a corps flourished. Many doors on which Commissioner Schurink had knocked remained open to the Army because of the integrity and involvement of Russian Salvationists.

Moldova, a small republic in the shadow of Ukraine which claimed independence from Russia when the Soviet Union broke up, was on Commissioner Schurink's list of potential openings. After a year in Kiev, Majors Wesley and Ruth Sundin were given a new challenge. They were to open Salvation Army work in Chisinau, the capital of Moldova. The official language was Romanian – the third foreign language the couple had to try to absorb.

Ruth's excitement about the way in which the power of God was felt spilled over into newsletters and reports by which she kept the whole world (almost!) informed. They began by telling Chisinau that The Salvation Army was in town by means of bold banners strung across a main street announcing the opening meeting. The prestigious Organ Hall had been hired and many people from Kiev, including a singing company, were on their way to share the celebration. Commissioner Schurink and Colonels Milford and Patricia Hickam were about to be briefed on the proceedings over a meal with the Sundins when a message came which pricked the balloon of anticipation. The Minister of Culture and Religion had prohibited the opening festival to be held the next evening.

Disappointed but not defeated, they tackled the problem first thing in the morning with the help of Pastor Slavak, a Baptist minister. Ruth Sundin reports: 'Wes, Commissioner Schurink and

Pastor Slavak visited government office after government office, trying to secure the clearance we needed to go ahead with the meeting. We continued our plans already set in motion, praying for God's intervention every step of the way. Of course, we had our opening meeting! We just could not call it such, and the government leader we had invited to speak did not do so. The success of our meeting was enhanced rather than hurt by this experience as 550 people crowded into the hall to hear the message. We certainly give God the glory for his continual intervention and support on behalf of our ministry.'

The momentum continued. Corps Secretary Claudia Babariaco became a key person supporting the Sundins, thus keeping their morale high. She had been a Christian for 40 years but as a woman had no opportunity to serve in the Moldovan Baptist Church she attended. She saw in the Army opportunity for her to express her gifts of hospitality and language. A thriving home league grew through Claudia and others like her caring for neighbours and friends.

Two Moldovan soldiers from Voronez, Oleg and Tatiana Morozov, became envoys and opened Botannica Corps, also in Chisinau. Although they left to train for officership the corps continued to grow.

Time came for the Sundins to take up a new appointment as regional officers based in St Petersburg, handing over their precious people to the care of Captains Will and Sue Cundiff. Having proved God in so many ways, they asked for even greater things – that Moldovans who were committed to Christ would seek to influence those in power. Dark forces still had control but Wesley and Ruth Sundin believed that 'thy Kingdom come' was not a vain dream, but a certain hope.

Looking back over eventful months as he approached the date of his official retirement, Commissioner Schurink mused on the 'great leap forward' he had been charged to make. 'This has only been partially accomplished,' he wrote. Yet he knew that even this was more than he could have expected to achieve. 'But for the Holy Spirit, I could never have managed. To God be the glory!' he added. Doors of opportunity were still standing open, and he prayed continually, 'The fields are white unto harvest. Lord, please send labourers.'

The buzz of excitement as Commissioner Schurink, heralded by smiling timbrelists, entered Presnia hall between rows of flag-waving junior soldiers on 22 June 1994 indicated the style of leadership the commander had given in the past two years. Although he had found no joy in spartan Russian living conditions, his exuberance in ministry was contagious. He was surrounded with friends who vied with each other to pay tribute in traditional Russian style with words and gifts. Perhaps the most moving gift was a simple wooden cross carved by Philip Rubakov who led his corps people in singing one of the commander's favourite songs, 'The old rugged cross'.

The commissioner's wife, Wietske, suffering from severe Alzheimer's disease and being cared for in The Netherlands, was not forgotten when Commissioner Ron Cox, retired Chief of the Staff, presented certificates marking the retirement of gifted, faithful Salvation Army officers. Commissioner Cox's thoughts flashed back to a conference in Sweden in 1987 when delegates pleaded with God to open doors for the gospel to move into the east. It had seemed impossible then.

'Don't forget us' . . . 'Pray for us!' These words were repeated over and over again as a queue moved slowly past Commissioner Schurink after the meeting to wish him farewell. 'I won't forget,' he confirmed. Nor will his people forget him and his influence on their lives.

Commissioner Schurink was departing but in answer to his prayers the Lord was sending labourers into this field. Lieut-Colonel Lucille Turfrey, Principal of the Institute for Officer-training, eagerly scanned the papers presented at each candidates board. Each set of papers told a moving story of challenge and

153

response to the call to officership. Applications came from every part of the command. Some heard God's call at youth councils which took place in every region in 1995. Others were inspired by the example of faithful officers. Eighty delegates who were seriously considering leadership attended a 'future service seminar' in 1996. Captain Wendy Walters, then responsible for preparing candidates, had a busy task guiding each applicant into the right path of service.

Mamuka and Eka Adhazava were among those who heard God's call for service. Eka had discovered Jesus through reading history as a child and attended the Orthodox Church in her teens with her mother. It was a formal experience and she understood very little of the liturgy.

Her husband, Mamuka, was totally in the dark about religion. His father was a staunch Communist. The boy felt no compunction about dabbling in criminal activity. They married in 1991 and in due time baby Katie was born. Three years after their marriage they saw an item on television about The Salvation Army which had come to Tblisi. They decided to go but just as they arrived they were almost dissuaded by a woman leaving the hall declaring that these people were crazy!

At first everything did indeed seem strange to Eka, whose memories of church were totally different from this informal gathering. Mamuka, however, was interested even though his previous reaction to religious believers had been mockery.

Family sickness and bereavement at this time brought such grief that Eka shut herself away, questioning a God who could allow her seven-year-old sister to die. Then she recalled that her sister had trusted God even in her sickness. Remorse for her doubting swept over Eka and she longed to possess her sister's faith. Returning to the Army, where Mamuka was preparing for soldiership, she found comfort and assurance. Her husband's life was so different and she felt that her own commitment to God and the Army would help them as a family.

The Nesterenkos nurtured the young couple lovingly, seeing potential in them now that God had changed their lives. They were given responsibility for an outpost, far away in Kutaisi. This was a testing time for them both but they learned to depend on God, seeking his guidance through the Bible and prayer. Now it was time to take another step. Sure of their calling to officership, they took the long journey to Moscow, leaving family and friends for a while.

The Institute for Officer-training had outgrown the space at the top of the headquarters building and another place was rented where the largest session yet could both live and study. Sadly, Lucille Turfrey had returned to Australia for medical treatment. The Vanovers had completed their term of service and returned to their home territory too. The new principal, Lieut-Colonel Sharon Berry, with Captains Mark and Jennifer Fagerstrom and Sandra Reid, had the daunting task of preparing the new premises which occupied the top floor of a sanatorium on the outskirts of the city.

When the 16 cadets of the Builders of the Kingdom Session arrived on 19 September 1996 from Moldova, St Petersburg, Kiev, Georgia and Moscow, they set to and finished the work and the session settled down to a purposeful training programme. There was no doubt that these young people would have a significant part to play in the building of God's Kingdom in their homelands.

When Commissioner Schurink left the Russia/CIS Command he handed his responsibilities to Colonels Brian and Carolyn Morgan. For these officers, who had revelled in established Salvation Army work in the hot climate of northern Australia, it was a daunting prospect to be asked to lead a new Army in frozen northern Europe. A grandchild had just been born and the thought of not being near enough to watch a new personality developing was painful. But the Morgans had never refused an appointment and the joy of seeing new Christians growing in Christ would be more than enough compensation for any hardship.

Whatever their fears (and naturally, there were many) these were soon dispelled by the warmth of Russian Salvationists and friends.

In their 'home' corps of Lublino, the Colonel's firm handshake, ready smile and *'Dobre deyn!'* greeting delighted his fellow worshippers, while in every part of the widespread command they were soon respected and loved.

Reports and briefings soon gave the colonel a picture of his responsibility. Establishing his place at the head of a team of strong personalities from a range of cultures when he was 'the new boy', was not easy. Cautiously, similar to the way he was learning to walk on icy pavements, he stepped out in faith and led the command forward. He had set his goals to consolidate work already begun, to continue expansion where personnel and finance allowed, to extend women's ministries, to evangelise and disciple and, above all, to develop national officers. Ministering to cadets on spiritual days at the college became a special privilege, challenging him to channel in the most effective way the potential he saw before him.

Coming from the United States, Evelyn LaBatte worked in the office with the Morgans and soon appreciated both their problems and their great reliance on God for solutions. She shared their faith. Coming to Russia because God had called her and then opened doors to make it possible, Evelyn became immersed in the Russian scene, appreciating its wealth and complexity, awed by its long history. As she explored Moscow's oldest streets, Edic, one of the young Russians accompanying her, would gleefully point out, 'And this was here before Columbus discovered America!'

Cadets, soldiers, visitors to command headquarters, fellow employees – all were cheered by her wide smile and positive words. Her past experiences were used by God. A former corps cadet counsellor, she led a corps cadet programme for young people of Moscow, by prayer seeking to guard them from Satan's power which seemed to cast a shadow on even the brightest experiences. A dressmaker, she tailored uniforms for cadets.

When she felt most alone in the great, alien city she sensed the light of God's presence in a very real way. Like her boss, Evelyn proved the power of prayer. It was her great joy to be accepted as an auxiliary-captain, answering a prayer which for many years had remained unfulfilled due to personal circumstances.

The Morgans soon knew that they were involved in a very active Army. Summer months saw service corps teams from abroad in action. Just before the teams arrived, the visit of the National Capital Band from Washington had made a great impression on musicians in St Petersburg, Moscow and Kiev as they lifted up the name of Jesus in prestigious open-air venues, encouraging corps to use similar opportunities while people were relaxing out of doors. The band had performed at the opening of St Petersburg West Corps which Adrian Allott had pioneered in his spare time from working on Army accounts at the St Petersburg office.

Things were happening down in Ukraine, too. A large group of Salvationists from Winton Corps in the UK, inspired by a visit from Sven Ljungholm some months previously, had worked toward and planned an expedition to Kiev. They were to support a summer music camp as well as bring a truckload of supplies which included a thousand tins of food given by local school children with their entries for a colouring competition, and many second-hand brass instruments which Winton juniors had helped to restore to their original brightness.

Soon after this event, which culminated in a joyful music festival and an enrolment of newly-trained soldiers, Sven and Kathy Lungholm said farewell at the end of their term as pioneers in Russia and Ukraine. They had expected great things from God when they picked up the thread of service left so long before by Sven's grandparents. God had indeed worked wonders in the lives of some fine Salvationists whose eyes had been opened to his reality through the ministry of the Ljungholms. It is an awesome responsibility to represent Christ to those who have never known him before.

The momentum of Commissioner Schurink's great leap of faith continued apace in the following months. As the Morgans travelled the command coping with the vagaries of weather, officialdom and transport, they were inspired by fine Russian Salvationists who exemplified the Army spirit as if they had been involved for years, not months. They were grateful for the tireless work of reinforcement officers living in an environment far removed from their roots. They perceived stresses which only came to the surface in the quietness of home after an encouraging day at a corps. Their cheerful presence and thoughtful prayer lightened burdens for those who were stationed many miles from other Army centres.

The crucial business of registration was slowly progressing. Early in 1995 Commissioner Lennart Hedberg, the International Secretary for Europe, joined Colonel Morgan and Captain Ron Lee when they met the Georgian minister for justice in Tblisi. They came away rejoicing at the news that the Army was registered as a Christian humanitarian aid group and registration as a church would follow.

Another success was reported at Rostov-on-Don. Lieutenants Geoff and Sandra Ryan had transferred to that city in the summer of 1994, handing over responsibility for St Petersburg Central Corps to American Lieutenants Alastair and Carol Bate. Three young Russian Salvationists, Vika, Tanya and Julia completed the planting team.

Unlike St Petersburg, the southern city of Rostov is far removed from Western influence. It is the heart of the influential Cossack region. The challenge of pioneering another new corps in the light of the past three years' experience, was an exciting one for Geoff and Sandra. By the new year an effective programme was in place, based at the Litsay Institute, where staff were most co-operative.

In April, the Morgans and UK officer, Major Rob Garrad, recently appointed Command Finance Secretary, witnessed the enrolment of the first two soldiers of the corps, a young married couple who were convinced that God's place for them was in The Salvation Army.

The Commander was moved to meet a young woman who had first been aware of Jesus through a painting. Visiting an exhibition of religious art, much of which had been hidden away for many years, Ira was arrested by a striking picture of Jesus. This young woman, whose thorough Communist training in the young Pioneers had kept her ignorant of the Bible, was moved to tears as she stood face to face with the 'unknown God'. Why did the picture have such a strange effect on her?

The mystery was solved when she visited the Army at Rostov. The whole focus of the meeting was on the person she had 'met' in the gallery. Hearing of his love for humanity which led him to death on a cross, Ira could understand why she had been so moved and she responded to that love, accepting salvation.

Confirmation that Rostov and its surrounding area was one of God's places for the Army came with official registration as a church. A lively, effective Sunday school and a modern expression of music confirmed that the Army's future in the city was promising. Geoff and Sandra, promoted to the rank of Captain that June, thanked God for his guidance and faithfulness.

Susan Harris, who later took an appointment as assistant at Rostov, led a team of young people from Moscow corps the following summer to engage in street ministry. With music, dance, testimony and Bible teaching they shared with Rostov Salvationists the joy of presenting the gospel to those who would listen. Social needs of the community were addressed too. With much planning and fund-raising a rehabilitation programme was set up and an experienced lay-Salvationist couple recruited to run it.

In spite of tremendous progress seen in all parts of the command it was wise not to become complacent. There were still those who resented the Army's presence and wanted to close the door against it once and for all. This became all too clear one weekend at Rustavi, Georgia, where Lieutenants John and Alison Norton were stationed.

A protest march by a large Orthodox group carrying misleading banners about The Salvation Army stopped outside the hall where the holiness meeting had recently concluded. Sunday school was in progress and an uneasy restlessness was felt. It was a potentially dangerous situation and it was important to act wisely and gently.

John calmed his people and then went out to meet the priests at the front of the procession, inviting them into the hall to discuss the problem quietly. To his relief, they agreed to this suggestion. Once inside, they set out their objections. They declared that the Army was not registered as a religious church, only as a charitable organisation. Long before, a government official in Tblisi had assured Captain Ron Lee that registration of both kinds would be no problem once the law was clarified. It still had not been processed. The Orthodox priests were quite correct.

Imparting the disturbing news that they would do their best to thwart the Army's evangelical ministry, the crowd dispersed. It was a sad episode. John and Alison led their congregation in prayer for understanding and tolerance between God's people. Then, using the wonder of email, a prayer request was sent around the world: 'Pray that the hearts of the Orthodox community will be softened by the Holy Spirit so that we can together find a way to co-operate. It is our desire to reach out in love to our Orthodox brothers and sisters, rather than condemn them.'

Far north of Georgia news of a more encouraging development had been received. Unknown to Army leadership, a corps had been seeded in Petrozavodsk, a city 300 miles north of St Petersburg. In 1994 a Christian from that city attended Salvation Army meetings in St Petersburg several times when on holiday. Impressed by what she saw, she felt led by God to open a corps at home.

The following February the woman appeared at regional office with an amazing report – and a request for an officer to pastor the congregation of 80 people who met for worship each Sunday! During those few months the 'unofficial Salvationist' had inaugurated Bible study, Sunday school, league of mercy and other welfare work. She did not ask in vain. Investigations confirmed her report. On Sunday 3 September 1995, Colonel Morgan installed

Captain Denise McGarvey as corps officer of Petrozavodsk. Terri Lines would leave her responsibility as youth co-ordinator in St Petersburg to assist Denise in this new venture.

Vladivostok, as far East as you can go in Russia, would soon be on the Army map too. The Korean Territory had it in its sights, just across the Sea of Japan. Captain Lee, Jung-hoon and his wife, Captain Park, Sun-re, with their daughter, Lee, Ji-eun and son, Lee, Hong-kyoo, were sent to the city with a brief to 'spy out the land' ready to open a corps after a few months. The Ah Hyun Corps, Seoul Division, was largely responsible for financing the venture, led by the corps sergeant-major who donated a very large proportion of the gift, having saved in response to the Holy Spirit's prompting. The mission, backed with prayer and faith, proved successful. Another chapter in the saga of The Salvation Army in Russia had begun.

EPILOGUE

THE metro offers welcome relief from stifling city streets in a Moscow summer. Commuters ease themselves into extra space, vacant because families have decamped to the countryside. They even have room to spread their newspapers.

A man in uniform, with *Armiya Spasseniya* on the cap-band, glances at a stark headline: 'State Duma supports religion bill.' It was not good news for The Salvation Army, nor for many other smaller churches. If the bill eventually reached the statute book it could severely restrict the freedom of religious minorities, each of which would have to apply for registration by the end of 1998 with proof that they had been in existence in Russia for at least 15 years. A more liberal law introduced in 1990 had allowed undesirable cults as well as widely-respected religious movements into the country. Now a sifting process was to begin.

Misha's Russian philosophy was wedded to a deep Christian faith. He knew from experience the wanton power of Russian politicians but he now firmly believed that God would have the final victory. Had he not had a glimpse of such a victory parade at the Jubilee Congress a matter of days before?

The first venue considered for the congress had proved to be too small once applications began to arrive from all parts of the Russia/CIS Command. Major Rob Garrad, who had responsibility for organising the event, at last secured a large hotel complex at Ismalova and preparations to celebrate the sixth anniversary of the Army re-entering St Petersburg, and the fifth since Moscow Central Corps opened again, went into full swing.

General Paul and Commissioner Kay Rader, whose keen interest in the command during their leadership of USA Western Territory had generated much practical support, travelled from London to celebrate with Colonels Brian and Carolyn Morgan, prospective Chief Secretary Lieut-Colonel Carl Lydholm and his wife Gudrun, from Denmark, and almost a thousand people from the command's four countries, Georgia, Moldova, Ukraine and Russia. Traditional folk ceremonies and song marked their differences but joyful, sincere Salvationism united them into one body. It was an exhilarating, inspiring occasion.

During the weekend 17 cadets of the Builders of the Kingdom Session were sent out with the challenge from Commissioner Kay Rader to be examples of God's love. They were going to plant new corps, to develop outposts or to support the ministry already in progress at existing corps. The lieutenants were a wonderful jubilee offering to the people of Russia and the CIS.

Often the venue resounded with music. Zürich Central Band shared its wealth of talent; harmonic and dramatic riches from within the command added to the joyful sound. Between sessions, informal groups made music in foyers and lounges, drawing delegates into a spirit of worship and praise. Abandonment in praise was matched with intensity in prayer and spiritual teaching. Many, moved by personal testimony and the interpretation of God's word, made new commitments to Christian living and opened the way for the Holy Spirit to work through them.

A number of officers and lay-workers from other territories who had served in the command returned to celebrate the jubilee. It was delightful to renew friendships and to observe evidences of progress and development. Others who could not make the journey found their thoughts constantly wandering during that weekend in May. Could it be true? Were there really hundreds of Russian, Moldovan, Georgian and Ukrainian Salvationists rejoicing together in Moscow, so recently forbidden territory for the majority of the world? 'Yes, it is true!' they confirmed to themselves. 'A miracle! A thousand miracles! And, praise God, I played a small part.'

Far away in Australia, General Eva Burrows(R) eagerly read reports of the congress. Every day she prayed for the former Eastern bloc countries which, as world leader of The Salvation Army, she had coveted for God's Kingdom. It was during her term of office that the longed-for yet unexpected opening of the door into Eastern Europe had come. Salvation Army leaders had investigated, experts had advised, financiers had juggled figures, and the reports came onto the General's desk. A decision – with many unknown ramifications – had to be made.

General Eva recalled the moment she had said 'Yes!' It had been right then and was right now. Using her office to appeal for resources, the response had been confirmation. Money flowed in, including a single donation of more than a million dollars from a woman with a great zeal for souls. Further confirmation came as dormant 'yellow, red and blue' flames in Hungary, Czechoslovakia, Latvia, East Germany and Russia were fanned into life once more. News of the jubilee commissioning lifted General Burrows's spirits. Sending out the first 10 new lieutenants in 1993, she had had faith to believe that others would respond to God's call – and indeed, they had.

But there could be no complacency in the war against evil, even at a time of jubilee. Prayer was needed more than ever. After the news from the Duma, General Rader issued a call to prayer to Salvationists worldwide. General Burrows, with thousands of others, continued to intercede day by day.

Misha stared at the headlines. As he did so, he could hear General Rader's voice echoing from the congress . . . 'Our fight is spiritual and God has provided the possibility for victory!' It was the word of confidence for the moment.

Leaving the train Misha struck up a conversation with a fellow passenger. His uniform had aroused her curiosity. These days military uniforms were not as frequently seen as five years previously. He began their conversation on the subject of The Salvation Army but it did not end there. He spoke of his personal experience of God and his friendship with Jesus. Grace is more relevant to Misha than law. With his fellow Christians he believes that no man, no law, can prevent a believer, saved through the sacrifice of Jesus, from entering the door of God's Kingdom.